MEGA BUILDER

ROBLOX

A COMPLETE GUIDE

30 YEARS®

TRIUMPH
B O O K S

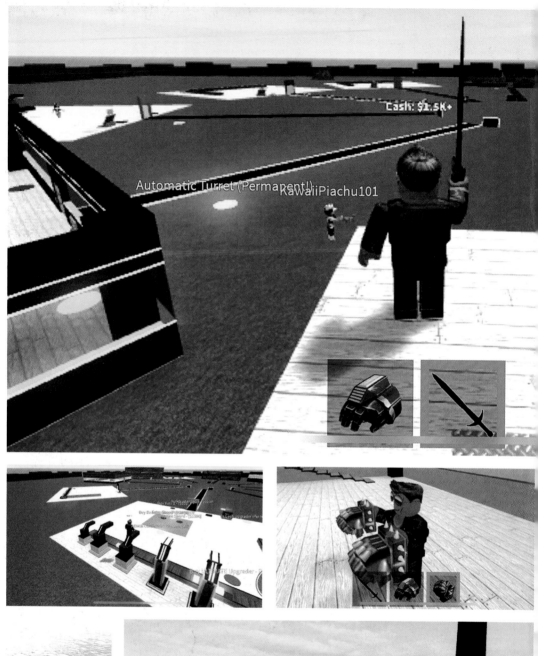

Automatic Turret (Permanent!)

KawaiiPiachu101

Cash: $1.5K+

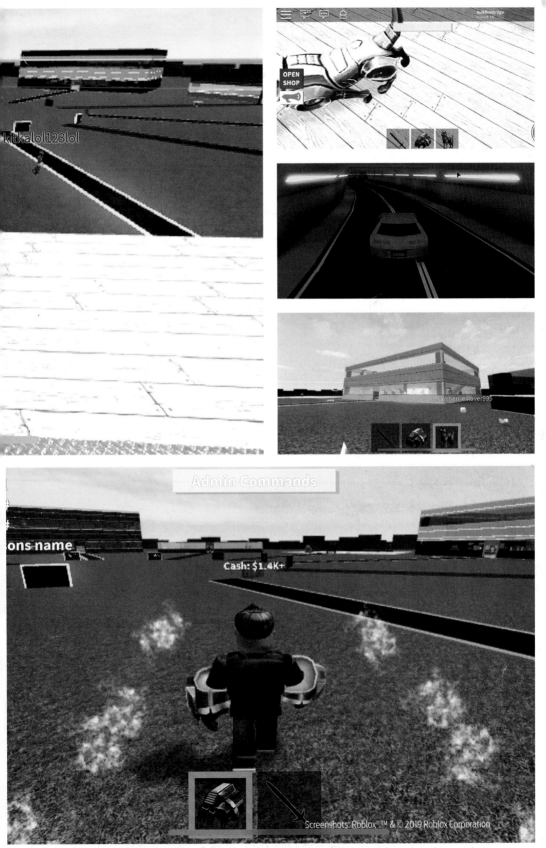

This book is book is available in quantity at special discounts for your group or organization. For further information, contact:

Triumph Books LLC
814 North Franklin Street
Chicago, Illinois 60610
Phone: (312) 337-0747
www.triumphbooks.com

Printed in U.S.A.
ISBN:978-1-62937-756-8

Content packaged by Mojo Media, Inc.
Joe Funk: Editor
Samantha M Skinner: Writer
Jason Hinman: Creative Director
Jack Hinman, Mia Hinman and Parker Hinman: Gaming Consultants
Janey Funk: Gaming Expert

Contents

ROBLOX

@badccvoid 11:30 AM

emscool223]: ##garage
emscool223]: #
emscool223]: o
oYoGuest0]: At dealership where monster truck is
P [beastofireandchath]: Oh
tphoenix]: dod
oYoGuest0]: I has trails when u buy and ride it
oYoGuest0]: It
oYoGuest0]: Are u afk
oYoGuest0]: Nvm
oYoGuest0]: Dont be afk or u miss the train
P [beastofireandchath]: My chat is #### right now it doesnt lemme talk

My chat

Bounty
$0

Expires in 11:40:23
Mission Progress...

Press & hold behind the backs

Screenshot: Roblox® ™ & © 2019 Roblox Corporation

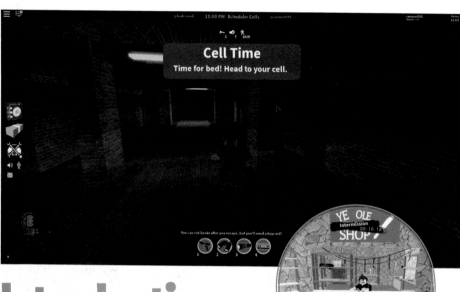

Introduction

Hello friend!

We are happy to have you here and talking about all that has changed about Roblox – and believe us, there have been A LOT of changes happening!

Roblox is the fun, exciting game that offers so much to online players.

Whether you've played Roblox before or this is your first time there's so much for you to do once you create your account. You can go into worlds, games, and other dimensions created by other users just like you! Some of them are free to join, others cost Robux.

You can create your own worlds, games, dimensions that you want other players to visit. You can charge them, or you can open it up as free play to the public. The choice is yours.

Roblox is a friendly game, one that you can use your imagination with, and it's a fun place to make new friends as well. It is a game that welcomes everyone, regardless of their age or where they are from. There's so much fun just waiting for you in the game.

If you enjoy putting things together, making games, or even just make-believe then this might be the online game that you're looking for. You can invite friends to come into your world, or you can work alongside them to create something amazing for the other players.

There is so much to create, do and explore throughout the many worlds of Roblox. With so many changes that have been made, it's time to learn what's different and how you can make the most of your time in Roblox.

Everyone is invited to try out the world that has welcomed so many into it. Everyone is invited to see for themselves how it is to create a video game that actually works. Regardless of the world you imagine, or how hard it seems to create, it can be done and it's a lot of fun once you get the hang of it!

The best part is that now that you can charge visitors Robux to come into the world, you have the ability to actually make some cash back! This is what so many kids are doing today, so we put together a full section on this idea in the book.

Everyone wants something to do and a game like Roblox that sparks the imagination, while allowing players to build, create and play, should keep players busy for a long time. The best part is that Roblox can be used on just about any platform now. They have expanded their base, so you can go beyond the computer. Take it to your gaming console, challenge someone on your Xbox.

So what else are you going to learn if you keep reading?

Let us give you a little insight on what we are prepared to offer you.

ROBLOX

If this is your first time playing, we will give you a nice little overview of what to expect, the basics of the game, how to play, where to play and more. This will just be a recap for those of you that are pretty much experts, but we shouldn't leave anyone out.

If you wanted to know where Roblox came from, and who developed it, we have you covered with a section in the book that really dives into that area as well.

You can create an awesome avatar, even more awesome then when the game first came out with the tips and tricks that we give you in this book. Take a look at how awesome we've made our avatar with simple tips like the ones we offer here.

How would you like to explore new and exciting places in Roblox? We'll cover some of the most awesome places that you go to play. We will give you a little bit of info on each one, and a quick snapshot, so you can have an idea of what to expect before you ever make your way into those worlds.

If you wanted to take advantage of the themed monthly events that happen every year, we will cover that as well. Who knew there was so much to do in the world of Roblox?

With over 30,000 new games added daily, will yours be one of them? This is an overview of the new games you can visit, what to expect with them and how you can make your own top playing game – through the tips and tricks that we provide right here for you to use.

Take a walk through the timeline of how Roblox has changed throughout the years and what it has done, as well as what the game makers want to do in the future.

We'll walk you through a tutorial of how to make your own game, as well as how to monetize it – who doesn't want to do something totally awesome and then get paid for it?

Then we can help you sell the game and get visitors, because it's fun to be on the front page when people come and go from the website. Reaching the front page is the best way to get your game noticed!

So how else can you earn Robux and then how can you spend it once you get it? That's another topic that we cover in this book.

Want to see Roblox in action in the news? We discuss some of the coolest things they have done so far with this pretty awesome game. It is a must see!

If you're interested in things like cool game facts, safety tips, advanced tips, tricks and hacks (from the pros, of course!) and a a bit of behind the scenes action, you can get all of that and more in this book as well. With our guide you'll learn a bit more about the top Roblox players and the worlds they've created and last, but not least, the Roblox toy line and all the different toys available today.

Our guide offers a bit of information on almost everything you can think of about the game, so you can learn what's most important to you about Roblox.

So many players love this online game and are inviting their friends to play. If you want to try it out, we invite you to. If you are one of the experts of the game, we salute you and encourage you to keep reading because we have some advanced stuff in here too!

Sneak peaks, never before seen events, awesome extras and more! We've put it all together for our fans and we want to make sure you get the awesome front seat needed to take advantage of all this information we've put together.

You have it now, you have it first, with our exclusive book put together just for you! ■

MEGA BUILDER

camscool223		Money	Miles Drive
Account: <13		26,660	1,526.37
Citizens		506,079	963.46
ferrari000999		356,051	649.81
zombub517		136,408	274.07
mtafan123		12,441	38.9
awesome112233ify		1,179	0.68
Criminals			
Police		50,719	13.53
atlas00056		50,719	13.53
Prisoners			
SWAT		26,660	1,526.37
camscool223		26,660	1,526.37
TowTruckers			
TransitDrivers			

Volkswagen Beetle

Compact   Toyota Supra

$20,000   Sport   Toyota AE86

$40,000   Suzuki GSX-R1000

Sport

Shelby Super Snake   Subaru BRZ

Shift

Q

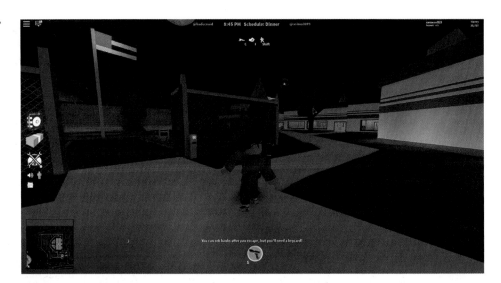

Overview of the Game

Even though some of us already know how to play Roblox, it is good to go over the basics for new players just getting started, and as a refresher for those that have been away for a long time.

With the game changing all the time, we want to make sure that you have some useful tips and tricks that will improve your experience now when you're building your own world and while you are playing in the worlds of others.

That's right...

You can visit your friends that have built a world of their own. Stop by and check out what they're doing and give them some feedback. You can use this time to tell them if they're headed in the right direction with their world too.

Roblox was made for everyone and you can play with friends that enjoy it just as much as you do!

THE BASICS OF GAME PLAY

Depending on where you're going to be playing Roblox, the controls of the game will change. This is something you'll get used to as you continue to play the game.

You can play on your Xbox system and use the controller to move your character and build your world.

If you are using your computer, then the keyboard and mouse are going to be all you need.

You can also play Roblox on your tablet or smartphone and you have all of the controls you need right on the screen. You just touch and go!

Free for All

Roblox is a FREE game to play, but if you want to go into some of the worlds then you may need to use Robux to get in and start playing. The people that make the games are able to charge an admission price to get in if they like, especially if they have a great game. You can do the same if you want! We will talk more about this later on in the book.

You have to sign up for a free account before you can start to play Roblox. You just need to visit the website and fill out the information in the box provided. Once you have an account, you can sign on and start playing.

Specific Requirements

Roblox will run on most computers and modern-day devices just fine. Most newer computers should be able to handle Roblox without an issue, and even many older machines will run the game well.

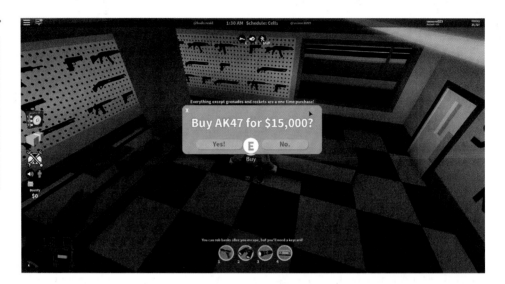

Windows Vista is recommended for computers or higher, though it will run on Windows XP. Those with Macs need version 10.7 or higher. Chrome OS is required, and most cellphones that are newer will support the play of Roblox and the builder.

Customization Options

You can customize your avatar and your profile, letting you make the most of all the modern extras that Roblox has to offer. Making these customizations makes it easier than ever for players to track you down. Creating an avatar that stands out is pretty fun to do. You can get cool swag for it such as awesome outfits and accessories that really up your style.

Controls and Playing the Game

To change the camera perspective, use the mouse and WASD and < > keys. With these buttons you can pan around the different sections and areas. Spending a bit of time getting used to the camera controls will make Roblox more enjoyable when you jump into the game. If you are not using a computer, then the joystick will allow you to look around and control your camera view.

Start your play session in Roblox by scrolling through the available games and selecting the one that looks the most appealing. You can play most Roblox games as soon as you understand how to pan around the camera, and move your character around. Learn those two things, and how to pick items and you'll be ready to play.

When joining a game in Roblox you'll often have access to gear in your character's backpack. Scroll through your available gear and select objects that you think will be most helpful. You can also just press the associated hotkey, usually numbers 1 – 6, to select the items you want as well.

Pressing / on your keyboard while playing the computer version opens up the chat bar. Simply type into this chat bar to talk with other players in the world. This allows you to win over some friends or make sure that the team you are a part of are all on the same page. There is also a choice to voice chat on all the different versions of Roblox, so you can talk with the other people playing the game in real time if you want.

ROBLOX

Roblox Badges

Veteran — Friendship — Homestead

Player Badges — See All

Thanks For Pla... — Halloween 2018 — A Watery Death — Welcome! — You Played Ve... — You played W...

Statistics

Join Date	Place Visits
3/8/2017	445

Badges Offered

There are all sorts of cool badges available to unlock in Roblox. You can earn badges during game play and when you become more familiar with the game. They don't give anything, but are pretty cool to collect and show off in your profile. The more places you visit and things you do in the game the more badges you can win.

Tutorials on Roblox

Some players have taken the time to create helpful tutorial games in Roblox that you can play around with as a new player. You join these simple tutorials just like you would a standard game, but they teach you useful techniques so that you can excel in Roblox. To make use of them, just join one of the tutorial worlds like you would with any other game, and walk around learning whatever it teaches. By going through a few tutorials you can master advanced concepts and get closer to being a real Roblox pro.

Here are just a few that you can join…

Fluffy_Joey's Tutorial
www.roblox.com/games/1296778083/tutorial

Andriano_Flores' Tutorial
www.roblox.com/games/1376954902/Tutorial

Kaixeleron's Tutorial
www.roblox.com/games/3004201/Roblox-
Tutorial-Legacy

Building on Roblox

The building section of Roblox is much more in-depth than playing games is. Fortunately, there is a builder tutorial available that will give you an idea of how to place everything, where you can find everything and basically how to create a full game without getting too overwhelmed.

The builder makes it easier than ever to build a world of your own. It's easier than it looks and you can literally create a full world in just minutes when you learn what you're doing. Do not become discouraged when you enter into the new space and see the huge number of options and tools. Each one is another useful tool that will help you create your next masterpiece, you just need to learn how they work. You can build with ease using these tools just by clicking on them. Many of the items are also drag and drop, making it much easier to build with.

It's true that the game packs in a huge number of options, but don't worry, you'll get comfortable with using them over time. Start playing with just a single tool or two, and slowly expand the number of tools that you use while creating worlds. Learning to use them takes time, but you'll be surprised by how quickly you pick up new skills with a bit of practice.

ROBLOX

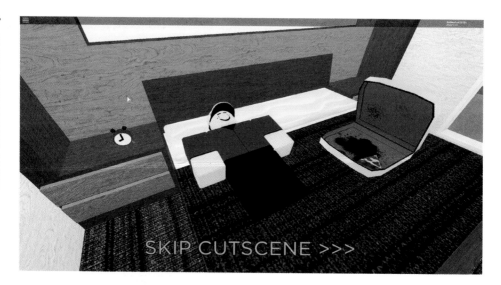

SKIP CUTSCENE >>>

There are many different tutorials that focus specifically on building in Roblox – for instance, our builder book provides insight on building just about any world you can think of!

We'll also offer some fresh building advice later on in this guide, so keep reading and you'll pick up some new exciting building ideas that you can use to create brand-new worlds in Roblox that everyone is sure to love!

Sign Up to the Builders Club

When you want to take your Roblox experience to the next level, and enjoy access to even more features, take a look at the Builders Club. The Builders Club is a premium version of Roblox that allows you to sell your creations to other players and to trade items. You'll also receive a specific amount of Robux every day. You get a different amount of Robux depending on the membership you decide on. Being a member of the Roblox Builders club also allows you to create Groups and to join more groups in the game. All these different features help make Roblox even more exciting, and the lower tier Builders Club memberships are surprisingly affordable.

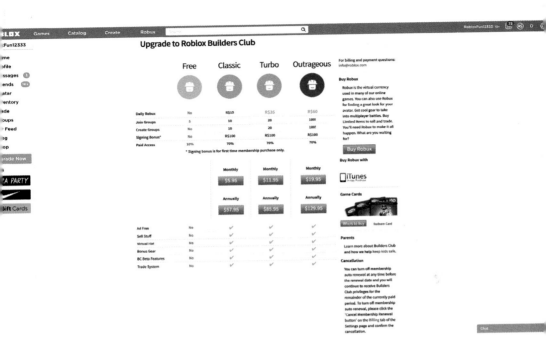

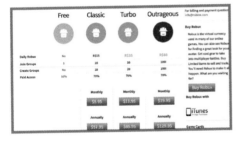

There are four tiers that you can sign up and become a part of.

FREE » CLASSIC » TURBO BUILDERS » OUTRAGEOUS BUILDERS

You can sign up for any of them based off of what you want to get and how much you want to pay. Everyone starts with the free account and you can upgrade from there.

Trading is Now Allowed

Previously, it was impossible to trade items between players in Roblox. This is something that has changed. Now you can swap items back and forth with your friends and have fun making trade deals with everyone you know!

Roblox is working hard to create a stronger in-game economy, and that means focusing on creating a better trading platform. Players will find trading simple and easy to do with just a bit of practice, and should be able to work toward the items they are most interested in. Roblox recently enjoyed a surge of new players and the creators are working hard to continue Roblox's growth for a bigger and more exciting game for everyone.

ROBLOX

With all these new platform changes, some older Roblox games are becoming outdated. That's why some of the classic games are no longer working. If you try and play an older game and it doesn't function that's because the world creators haven't updated their game to work with the new platform. If you run into this issue try messaging the creator letting them know about the issue. Some creators are actively working to get their games running once again, so some of your old favorites might become functional again.

Roblox is likely to continue growing for a long time. This is good for the game and it means you'll have new and exciting experiences for years to come!

WHY SHOULD YOU PLAY?

There are so many reasons why you should play. Here are just a few of our favorites. Read through them to decide if this is the game for you.

- Everyone plays Roblox! We are not kidding — everyone that is anyone plays Roblox. If you ask your friends, your neighbors, every kid that rides your bus — most of them are going to say that they play Roblox!

- You are creative, and you want to try to create something completely unique and that is all your own – Roblox has just the area for you to build as much, or as little, as you would like.

- You want to go into a world where you are able to socialize, meet new friends and people and have a great time.

- You want to explore new worlds and try out fun new games that were just created.

- You want to make a world and make Robux off that world. This is one of the best things about the game and if you create something truly unique you might be able to become a Roblox millionaire!

- You want a wide variety of different games to choose from, all with different designs and playstyles. You'll never be bored while playing the games and you can switch through them as many times as you want.

ROBLOX

- You can take advantage of the yearly events that the makers of Roblox put on. They put on the events in exciting new games and even give you a chance to cash in on some pretty sweet Roblox swag.

- If you love customizing characters and everything about them – there is a whole spot for this with countless outfits and looks to choose from.

- Last, but not least, it is free to play! If you don't have money to pay for a new video game, you don't have to worry. You have access to many games that are player made and free to enter and play at your own will.

Roblox is safe, it is fun, and everyone is welcome to come in and create a player to have fun with. Try it for yourself and you might learn some programming and game design skills during your time on Roblox. It's truly an all-in one game, and it's powerful enough to replace most other games that you can play today. There are literally pages and pages of games to choose from, and new ones are being added all the time!

Even if you don't see a reason here that appeals to you, Roblox is meant for everyone. You can jump on and see for yourself just how great the games can be and what sort of experiences await you.

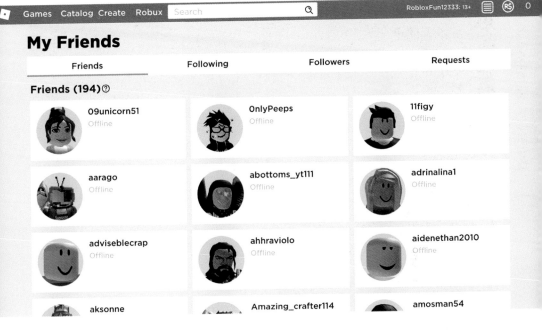

WHO PLAYS ROBLOX?

Those that play Roblox are the elite, the cool kids, the ones that understand how to have fun and how to be creative.

Of course, if you want to know who all is playing Roblox, then here are some ways to find your friends or just find new friends on Roblox.

Adding Friends You Know

If you know someone that plays Roblox, it's easy adding them to your friends list. Just go to the Home page, hit the icon at the top of the page with the person and the plus sign and type in the name of the person you want to add. Once the name is added in their profile should pop up on the screen, and you can add them to your list. If their profile doesn't show up, double check that you typed the name in right. Even a small spelling mistake will keep you from seeing your friends!

Finding New Friends on the Game

Go into games and use the chat box function to start chatting with people. You can make friends easily this way. A lot of times they will want to partner up and learn more about you and you can then add each other on the friends list for Roblox. You can add them the same way as above, or you can go to their profile when you click on their name and click to add them to your friends list. They just have to accept the request and you both will become friends.

ROBLOX

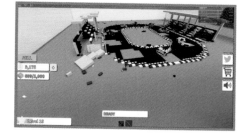

Having lots of Roblox friends is a good thing. You can add any friends to a game that you want and invite them to a party. It's simple joining the same worlds as your friends, and you'll be playing alongside them in no time.

Remember! You can only add up to 200 friends at a time into your account, so keep this in mind while you are adding people! Once it is full, you cannot add any more friends until the others are removed from the list.

Anyone and everyone plays Roblox. Even if you don't think they play, make sure to ask them. So many people play that you don't realize, but you'll never find them if you don't ask!

Swap names with your friends today and add them as a friend on your account! You can play in any of the worlds together or create your own and visit each other's.

WHAT YOU CAN DO IN THE GAME
There are so many things that you can do in Roblox. From playing in other people's worlds to creating your own and spending hours customizing your character. Many find building the characters one of the most exciting things that can be done.

RobloxFun12333

Friends	Followers	Following
194	586	0

About	Creations

bout

urrently Wearing

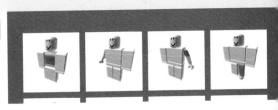

Roblox has had some exciting new changes that were made to the game that really make it stand out compared to the old style – instead of those old block characters that Roblox first came out with you have something more realistic to play with. The classic characters are still available if you like them, but you have more options now!

How do these characters differ from the originals?

The avatars for the game are changing and they are becoming more 'people' looking and less blocky.

The avatars have come a long way in what they can do and the changes you can make to them. You can customize your characters in many new and exciting ways, something that you could never do with the original Roblox game.

You can choose different clothes, hair styles, facial expressions, jewelry, and a bunch of other extras to deck out your character. If you want something specific, you just have to add Robux to your account and you can purchase whatever you want.

When you're choosing your look and outfit, you can switch the cameras between 2D and 3D, which gives you a different perspective to help you get just the right look.

Woman Torso

By ROBLOX ✓ Item Owned

This item is not currently for sale.

Edit Avatar

Type	Torso
Genres	All
Description	No description available.

Try On 2D

⭐ 95K+

You have so many options to go with that you can make your person look any way that you would like. You can change their skin color, the shape of their head, what they are wearing, the shape of their body and more.

Customize the character as much (or as little) as you want.

Throw Yourself into Friend-Made Worlds
Roblox is so amazing because of all the different creators working to build beautiful and exciting worlds. These immersive 3D worlds are in any theme you can think of, and they're a fun expression of imagination. Each world is created by an actual person with a fun idea, and by doing some exploring you can see what everyone else is coming up with.

There are literally thousands of different worlds to choose from. Some made from all new ideas, and others remakes of someone else's ideas. Either way, you have a lot of new places to explore and to play around with.

You can't explore every world created by others, because many cost Robux to visit, but there are countless free worlds for you to explore. If a world is free to play you'll see a green button on their page to play.

⚔ NEW MAP!⚔
Dungeon Quest

👍 92%   👤 28K

Mad City 👑
PYRAMID HEIST

👍 77%   👤 37K

Jailbreak 🍎
HELI BOMBS 🍎

👍 88%   👤 26.4K

[/e sit +
Elevator Fix]

👍 87%   👤 17.9K

Royale🏰 Hig

👍 88%   👤 2!

Top Rated

See All

The options that cost money will tell you how many Robux you're going to need in order to enter and play.

There is also a small area below the game that shows you how many people visit each of the games and how many people have liked the game. This gives every player, especially new ones to the game, an idea of how they might like the game based off of what other people that have played think of it. The more players and thumbs up the game has, the better the game is thought to be. This also boosts the game and puts it to the top of the list to be advertised to other players that want to play.

When you're first starting out, use player reviews and the number of players to help you decide on games to try. You can also use the search box at the top of the page to search up key words or phrases of things you like.

For instance – you can add in 'prom' or 'date' to be sent to a high school party. You can also put in 'shopping' or 'make over' and get sent to the games that allow you to play dress up and go shopping in malls. If you like animals, then putting 'pets' or 'zoo' in the search field will bring up many animal results for you to play.

With so many endless options available, you can find the perfect game for you with just a bit of searching.

Create Your Own World Easily

Roblox is designed for simplicity, and most of the building tools are drag-and-drop for this reason. You can move and put down everything you need and want in the world that you are creating when you use the Roblox builder to your advantage.

Instead of needing complex coding skills to make a world, Roblox has made it easier than ever for kids (like you!) to make their own games fast and easy.

It takes time to get comfortable with the tools but spending a bit of time practicing will give you all the experience you need to create beautiful worlds.

The creative mode of the game is what brings a lot of the players in. Everyone wants to create their own video game and Roblox is the game that lets you do just that. The best part is that Roblox makes it easy for kids like you to earn cash for your worlds as well, so you can profit from your creativity!

Do you think you could make a world that people will pay to visit?

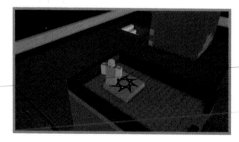

If you're not sure what that is yet, then we will help!

Roblox has so much to offer to everyone, even many parents have a good time on the different games offered. Everyone loves the changes that were made to the game, and the new events make Roblox an even more enjoyable experience.

We are going to do some shout outs at the end to some of my favorite players, as well as those that are at the top of their game and creating some of the best worlds out there. These guys are making the the top producing worlds out there that so many other players like to visit.

If you think you have what it takes to provide everyone with a world that they want to spend time in, then we invite you to keep reading our book. We'll explore some of the best areas in all of Roblox and give away some of the best money-making tips to help you make the most of every world that you create! We can even help give you ideas of what to build when it's time to make your first world.

Roblox is set to change in a big way this year. With the new look comes new fun and new experiences as well. Enjoy the new changes and choose games that speak to you – **or create your own games and amass your own Robux fortune!** ∎

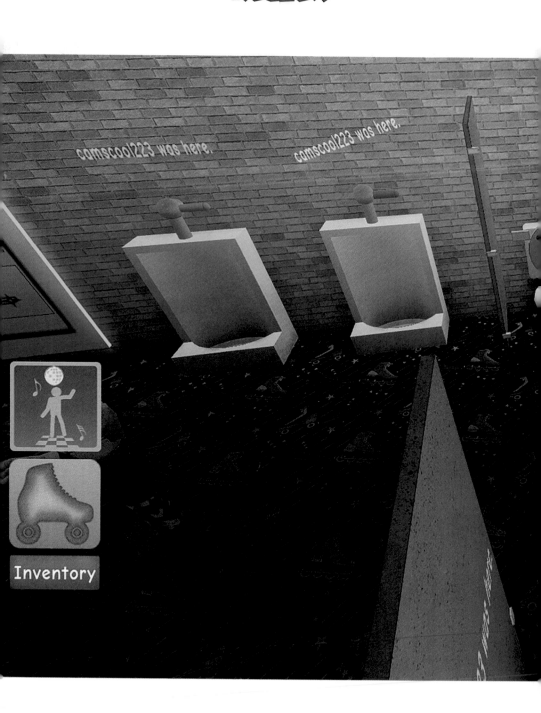

Inventory

ROBLOX

What Exactly is the History of Roblox?

Created in 2005, Roblox has long been a favorite game for so many kids. It took some time to get noticed, like most great games, but once it did it quickly gained ground as a top game for children and adults to explore.

The best part is that the idea was actually developed, but never pushed through, back in 1989. The makers of Roblox created something known as Interactive Physics. This is the framework and main idea of Roblox, but not as involved and developed as the game is today – and definitely not as successful as the finished product!

Roblox has come a long way in the years since it first started. It began as a PC-only gaming experience but has since expanded to countless other consoles and mobile devices.

Developed by David Baszucki and Erik Cassel, they decided to take the internet by storm using this awesome online gaming platform that welcomes kids of all ages to come in and do a little pretend playing.

If you like dressing up, pretending, creating and having fun with friends – Roblox is the game for you!

Introduction of Roblox Currency

Roblox Points were used when the game was first developed instead of the Robux we're familiar with today. Points were used for much more basic purposes than what Robux are used for today.

*Tickets weren't yet released when Roblox was first released, and this currency was short lived in the game.

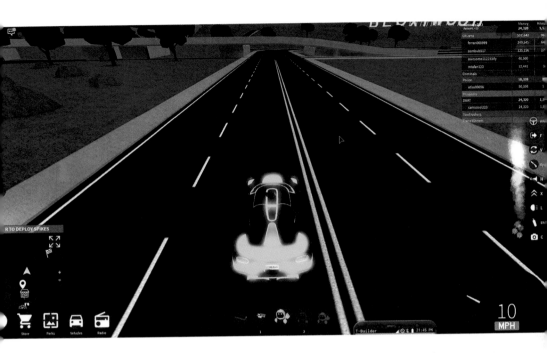

The Builders Club

The Builders Club was released in 2007 and continues to grow each and every day. This premium service expands with new members each month and has become more feature-rich as well. The Builders Club started with a single level, but now offers three different tiers, all with different perks to offer.

Introduction of the Trading System

The trading system was implemented back in 2012, but the early version was difficult to use for players. Most players didn't even know that trading was available early on. This difficulty encouraged the developers to create something more functional, and that wasn't released until only just recently. The original trading system only allowed premium members to trade premium items between one another, but the current model works for everyone.

Roblox was Hacked Back in 2012

By 2012 Roblox had a massive player community, but many of those players had no idea that the game was hacked by a team of hackers during this period. The hackers were searching for information about the players and the Roblox system. In response to the hack, the makers of the game took it offline to patch and fix any holes that might allow hackers to come back in and take more information.

Screenshots: Roblox® ™ & © 2019 Roblox Corporation

ROBLOX

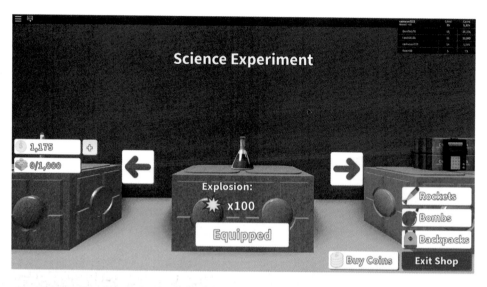

They learned who the hackers were, and they terminated them from the game and banned their IPs for good. This put the players' minds at ease, making it easier to have a good time the next time they logged in.

Sadly, in 2013, one of the original founders of Roblox passed away from his battle with cancer. Erik Cassel was no longer with the game or the world and the game paid tribute to him in its own special way.

Text filtering was introduced in 2016 after there were thoughts that the game was not safe for users under the age of 13. These chat filters were made to take out bad language and to make it safer for younger players to have a good time while online and to help keep them safe, without having to worry about the risks of online chatting.

In the years since its release, Roblox has gained millions of users and has been played by many big names in the gaming industry. It continues to grow with time and provide the users with a great experience. Since its original release, Roblox has had conventions, events and other exciting extras, all in response to the incredibly popular game.

Quick Cool Facts

Wondering a bit more about this awesome game and all that comes with it?

We have you covered!

Here are some pretty awesome quick facts we put together just for you! Some of them you might already know, just because you're pretty awesome yourself, and hopefully some will be new and exciting for you.

· At one point, there were over 1 million users on Roblox at the same time – imagine how many people you could have met that day!

· The top games can see around 20,000 visitors at once, all enjoying the same exact fun experience.

These events and conventions continue to this day, welcoming many of the big names in the gaming industry. If you're interested in these, you can check them out on YouTube or even visit them for yourself with help from a parent!

There is even a whole toy line that avid players and those that love Roblox can purchase, play with or collect for themselves!

ROBLOX

- There are around 180 million accounts on Roblox right now, but a lot of them are bots or alts that may not be used by regular people, like you and I.

- MMOG is what type of game Roblox is considered, which stands for Massively Multiplayer Online Game.

- The Roblox logo changed a bunch of times before they decided on one that they liked – even still they changed it over the past few years again!

- There are currently over 15 million games created by other players on Roblox and the number keeps growing!

- Roblox is rated as the #1 gaming website for kids and teens, especially those that like to talk to friends and build.

- Roblox is made up entirely of fully 3D models and worlds.

- Roblox is valued at around $2.5 billion.

- There's a virtual catalog that Roblox players can shop in to purchase different items for their avatar.

- Lua 5.1 is the coding program that Roblox uses to help users create their own worlds. It is a simple, easy to use language and works alongside a visual editor to make creating new game worlds simple and fast.

- It is possible to make cash off of the worlds you build in the game.

- There are players of Roblox that have become famous because of their playing within the worlds, and you have the strong possibility of creating something great and being noticed too!

- You can create groups and clubs within Roblox with other players. The biggest known group was RA or Russian Army.

Quick Grab & Go Info!
Website: www.Roblox.com
Release Date: 2005
Headquarters: San Mateo, CA
Creators: David Baszucki & Erik Cassel
Where to Play: Windows, iOS, Android, Xbox One, MacOS, Oculus Rift & HTC Vive

Roblox is a unique online game in the way it does things, but it's constantly changing and adding more features as well. What makes Roblox so special though is that they listen, so when you make a comment or give feedback – they can hear you and they might just change what you recommend! ■

SELL

$ 1,175 +

813/1,000

SELL

SHOP

Creating Your Avatar

Creating a person that really stands out and that shows everyone who you are and what your personality is can be an important task when getting started with Roblox. Fortunately, it's completely possible thanks to a powerful editor and item system!

Show off your unique style by making careful adjustments in the editor and you can go out into the Roblox worlds and get noticed by others.

Want pink hair? Need a shaved head? Want to wear something outrageous or perhaps something a bit more conservative?

The avatars in Roblox give you the creative freedom to dress how you want, look how you want and be who you want to be.

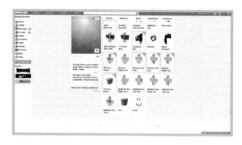

The first step is to locate your avatar on the home screen of Roblox. Once you've done that you can easily open the editing tool and adjust your avatar to look just the way you want. Once you have your avatar set up it's time to dress them up to complete your custom look. The sky is the limit when it comes to adjusting your avatar!

Start by selecting whether you want a boy or girl avatar and adjust your look from there.

When you are finished forming your new avatar you can work on dressing them up. The clothes you have to choose from depends on what is currently available in the catalog. You're free to be creative and make a statement with the clothing options offered in Roblox, and there are more than enough choices to let you create any style you like for your avatar.

DRESSING YOUR AVATAR

Select your avatar's picture on the front home page of the website. Once you do that you can then see what your avatar is currently wearing. This is where you can see them model any of the items you choose to put on them.

You can also click on specific areas of their body to change out what you want them to wear or how you want them to look in that area.

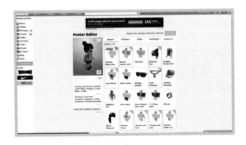

To dress or change out the clothing on the avatar, just scroll down past their body until you see the section for your inventory. Click on the inventory and you'll come to different clothing selections.

You will have a list of item categories to your left that you can click on. This will bring you to the items that you have for that specific category.

Go down the list and click on the categories that you want to change – pants, shirts, heads, animations, accessories, T-shirts and more.

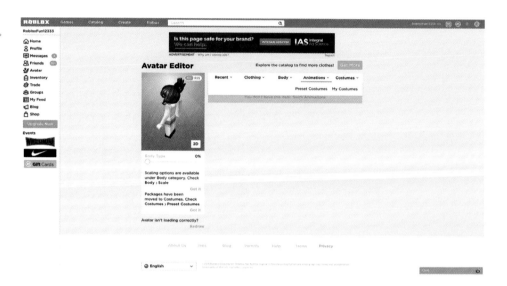

Once you have found the items that you want to put on your avatar, you just have to click on them and then click on the "Edit Avatar" button.

You will be able to see all of the available pieces and clothing that are in your inventory in the next screen. Select what you want to dress your avatar in here.

Click the items to add them to your avatar and click them again to take them off.

This is also where you can find all of your costumes, your animations, your expressions and change out the skin tone and color of your avatar. Every customization option for the character you have can be found in this area.

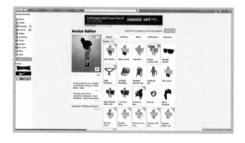

Once done customizing your avatar you just need to go to the home page again and you are ready to make use of your newly dressed up avatar. Now select a game you want to play or go to the builder to start building your own world.

If you want more to choose from than the clothing items you won, take a look at the items in the dressing catalog where you can find just about anything and everything you can think of!

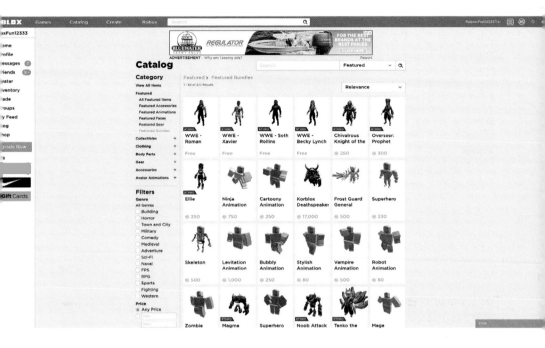

THE DRESSING CATALOG – WHAT'S AVAILABLE FOR PURCHASE

The catalog has much more than clothing and accessories that you can purchase for your avatar. You can purchase body parts that look different, animations for your avatar to use and even collectibles that you can show off in your collectible gallery on your profile.

The catalog is located at the top bar on the website. Simply click 'Catalog' and you're sent to the available options.

There are so many different items available for purchase here. With so many options, you may want to stock up on those Robux because that is how you purchase different outfits and looks!

If you are looking for something more specific for your avatar, there is a search box located at the top of the page. Click this box and type in the type of clothing you're looking for and then press Enter. This will bring you to the options that match your search with the most relevant placed at the top.

Let's Explore the Catalog in More Detail...

The catalog started off small but grows with each passing day as more and more player-made items to choose from are added on. You can even make and sell your own creations if you don't feel like spending Robux on something someone else made.

On the left-hand side where the different categories are, you'll see each of the following options to choose from:

- **View All Items**
- **Featured – All, Accessories, Animations, Faces, Gear, Bundles**
- **Collectibles**
- **Clothing**
- **Body Parts**
- **Gear**
- **Accessories**
- **Avatar Animations**

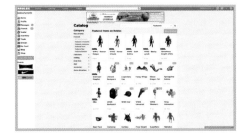

These categories break down even more, so you can find exactly what you're looking for for your avatar.

All of the catalog options have to be paid for, so you'll only want to take the time to shop if you have some Robux to spend.

Item prices depend on how much the maker of the item sets on them. While shopping you can sort your searched items by lowest or highest price or see them ordered by relevancy instead. This makes it easy to find items you can afford to buy.

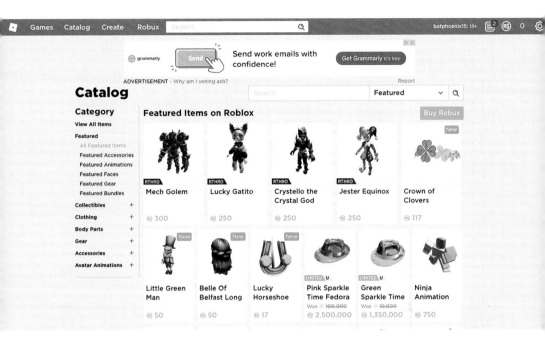

The items also have information on the developer of the items. This provides you with more information on who has made the item, but also gives you a list of the other items they have made in the past. This allows you to find many favorite items from the same developer easily.

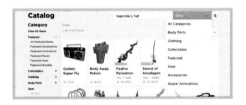

The search tool makes it easy for you to find those items that truly stand out.

Here are some pretty awesome catalog ideas and clothing options you can go with for your avatar!

ROBLOX CLOTHING CATALOG GALLERY

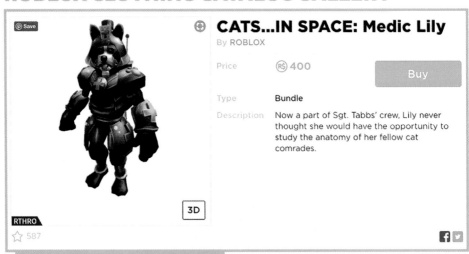

📌 Save

⊕ **CATS...IN SPACE: Medic Lily**
By ROBLOX

Price	®400
Type	Bundle
Description	Now a part of Sgt. Tabbs' crew, Lily never thought she would have the opportunity to study the anatomy of her fellow cat comrades.

Buy

3D

RTHRO

☆ 587

WHERE TO FIND IT:
Featured Items, All Featured Items

NAME OF DEVELOPER:
ROBLOX

WHAT IT IS:
Cats in Space, Medic Lily Set

WHERE TO FIND IT:
Featured Items, All Featured Items

NAME OF DEVELOPER:
ROBLOX

WHAT IT IS:
Digital Artist Bundle

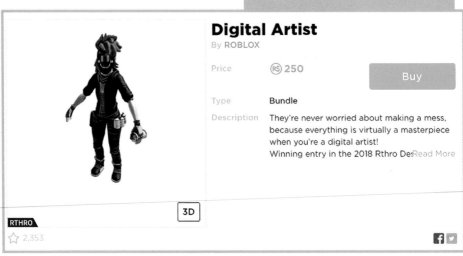

Digital Artist
By ROBLOX

Price	®250
Type	Bundle
Description	They're never worried about making a mess, because everything is virtually a masterpiece when you're a digital artist! Winning entry in the 2018 Rthro De Read More

Buy

3D

RTHRO

☆ 2,353

Black Wings
By ROBLOX

Price	(R$) 1,000
Type	Accessory | Back
Genres	All
Description	He may be flying solo- but at least he's flying!

Buy

Try On | 3D

☆ 148K+

WHERE TO FIND IT:
Featured Items, All Featured Items

NAME OF DEVELOPER:
ROBLOX

WHAT IT IS:
Black Wings

WHERE TO FIND IT:
Collectibles, All Collectibles

NAME OF DEVELOPER:
ROBLOX

WHAT IT IS: The Classic Roblox
Fedora (LIMITED ITEM)

The Classic ROBLOX Fedora
By ROBLOX

Best Price	(R$) 59,000
	See more Resellers
Type	Accessory | Hat
Genres	Adventure
Description	A black felt fedora. Ideal for 1920s journalists, detectives, and Linux hackers. This hat demonstrates good taste and exudes class.

Buy

Try On | 3D

LIMITED
☆ 52K+

Deluxe Game Headset
By ROBLOX

Best Price	ⓡ 1,960
	See more Resellers
Type	Accessory | Hat
Genres	All
Description	The perfect headset for chatting with your friends while playing games and looking cool!

Buy

Try On   3D

LIMITED
☆ 38K+

WHERE TO FIND IT:
Collectibles, All Collectibles

NAME OF DEVELOPER:
ROBLOX

WHAT IT IS: Deluxe Game Headset
(LIMITED ITEM)

WHERE TO FIND IT:
Clothing, Shirts

NAME OF DEVELOPER:
Purpose Tour

WHAT IT IS:
Fortnite Battle Royale Hoodie

💯 NEW 🔥 Fortnite Battle Royale Hoodie
By Purpose Tour

Price	ⓡ 57
Type	Shirt
Genres	All
Updated	Jan. 24, 2019 (by AsianGoku)
Description	Shirt

Buy

Try On   3D

☆ 724

CREATING YOUR AVATAR

MEGA BUILDER

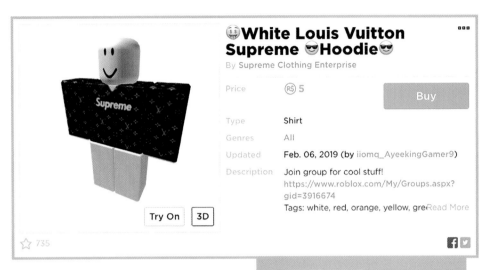

😃White Louis Vuitton Supreme 😎Hoodie😎
By Supreme Clothing Enterprise

Price	® 5
Type	Shirt
Genres	All
Updated	Feb. 06, 2019 (by iiomq_AyeekingGamer9)
Description	Join group for cool stuff! https://www.roblox.com/My/Groups.aspx?gid=3916674 Tags: white, red, orange, yellow, greRead More

Buy

Try On | 3D

☆ 735

WHERE TO FIND IT:
Clothing, Shirts

NAME OF DEVELOPER:
Supreme Clothing Enterprise

WHAT IT IS:
Louis Vuitton Supreme Hoodie

WHERE TO FIND IT:
Clothing, Pants

NAME OF DEVELOPER:
Sugardoll

WHAT IT IS:
Denim Jeans

♥ DENIM JEANS + FISHNET ♥
By sugardoll

Price	® 64
Type	Pants
Genres	All
Updated	Mar. 12, 2019 (by sugardose)
Description	match with | ♥ black off-the-shoulders ♥ https://www.roblox.com/catalog/1979333253/

Buy

Read More

Try On | 3D

☆ 2,644

Amory the Undead Necromancer

By ROBLOX

Price	(R$) 250

Buy

Type — Bundle

Description — A wizard boy who accidentally turned himself into a skeleton due to failed magic. Winning entry in the 2018 Rthro Design Contest. Created by xxthesmittenkittenxx2.

3D

RTHRO

☆ 11K+

WHERE TO FIND IT:
Clothing, Bundles

NAME OF DEVELOPER:
ROBLOX

WHAT IT IS:
Amory the Undead Necromancer

WHERE TO FIND IT:
Clothing, Bundles

NAME OF DEVELOPER:
ROBLOX

WHAT IT IS:
Skeleton

Skeleton

By ROBLOX

Price	(R$) 500

Buy

Type — Bundle

Description — The toe bone's connected to the foot bone, The foot bone's connected to the ankle bone, The ankle bone's connected to the leg bone ....etc etc etc

3D

☆ 3,675

Star-Mist Fairy
By ROBLOX

Price	Ⓡ 250
Type	Bundle
Description	From the depths of the galaxy, a fairy named Misty appeared. Her Crystal Clear Constellation wings hold the secrets of the universe, and her Starry eyes and St Read More

Buy

3D

RTHRO
☆ 5,226

WHERE TO FIND IT:
Clothing, Bundles
NAME OF DEVELOPER:
ROBLOX
WHAT IT IS:
Star-Mist Fairy

WHERE TO FIND IT:
Body Parts, Heads
NAME OF DEVELOPER:
ROBLOX
WHAT IT IS:
Chiseled

Chiseled
By ROBLOX

Price	Ⓡ 300
Type	Head
Genres	All
Description	A new shape for a timeless look.

Buy

Try On   3D

☆ 4,506

Screenshots: Roblox® ™ & © 2019 Roblox Corporation

ROBLOX

Shiny Teeth
By ROBLOX

Price	®35
Type	Face
Genres	All
Description	I brush my teeth 9 times a day to keep them extra sparkly!

Buy

Try On

☆ 149K+

WHERE TO FIND IT:
Body Parts, Faces

NAME OF DEVELOPER:
ROBLOX

WHAT IT IS:
Shiny Teeth

WHERE TO FIND IT:
Body Parts, Faces

NAME OF DEVELOPER:
ROBLOX

WHAT IT IS:
Friendly Smile

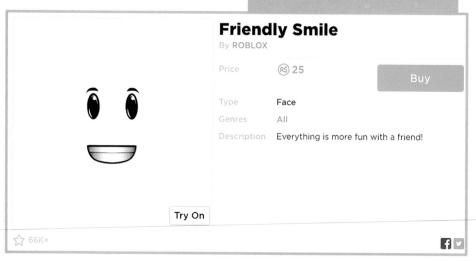

Friendly Smile
By ROBLOX

Price	®25
Type	Face
Genres	All
Description	Everything is more fun with a friend!

Buy

Try On

☆ 66K+

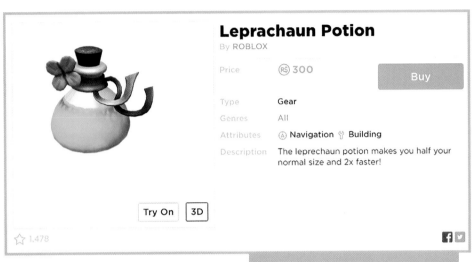

Leprachaun Potion
By ROBLOX

Price	(R$) 300	**Buy**
Type	Gear	
Genres	All	
Attributes	Ⓐ Navigation ⚡ Building	
Description	The leprechaun potion makes you half your normal size and 2x faster!	

Try On   3D

⭐ 1,478

WHERE TO FIND IT:
Gear, Building

NAME OF DEVELOPER:
ROBLOX

WHAT IT IS:
Leprechaun Potion

WHERE TO FIND IT:
Gear, Explosive

NAME OF DEVELOPER:
ROBLOX

WHAT IT IS:
Big Apple Launcher

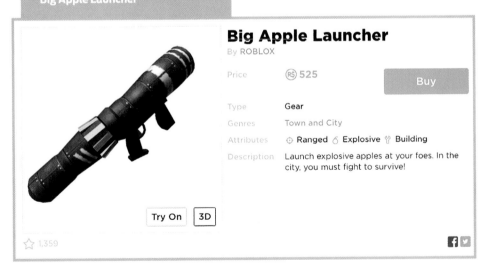

Big Apple Launcher
By ROBLOX

Price	(R$) 525	**Buy**
Type	Gear	
Genres	Town and City	
Attributes	⊕ Ranged 💥 Explosive ⚡ Building	
Description	Launch explosive apples at your foes. In the city, you must fight to survive!	

Try On   3D

⭐ 1,359

ROBLOX

ROBLOX World Tour Lightning Guitar
By ROBLOX

Best Price	ⓡ 850
	See more Resellers
Type	Gear
Genres	All
Attributes	🎵 Musical
Description	ROBLOX is kicking off our world tour and it's gunna be loud! This slammin' lighting guitar will send lightning at anyone nearby is you can play the notes just right.

Buy

Try On · 3D

LIMITED
☆ 1,874

WHERE TO FIND IT:
Gear, Musical

NAME OF DEVELOPER:
ROBLOX

WHAT IT IS:
ROBLOX World Tour Lightning Guitar

WHERE TO FIND IT:
Gear, Power Up

NAME OF DEVELOPER:
ROBLOX

WHAT IT IS:
Magic Ninja

Magic Ninja
By ROBLOX

Price	ⓡ 130
Type	Gear
Genres	Fighting
Attributes	🔱 Power Up
Description	The magic ninja will camouflage you to look like whatever you throw it at.

Buy

Try On · 3D

☆ 13K+

Doge
By ROBLOX

Price	ⓇⓈ 250
Type	Accessory | Hat
Genres	All
Description	Very hat. Such doge. Wow.

Buy

Try On | 3D

☆ 92K+

WHERE TO FIND IT:
Accessories, All Accessories

NAME OF DEVELOPER:
ROBLOX

WHAT IT IS:
Doge

WHERE TO FIND IT:
Accessories, All Accessories

NAME OF DEVELOPER:
ROBLOX

WHAT IT IS:
Scorpio Scorpion Tail

Scorpio Scorpion Tail
By ROBLOX

Price	ⓇⓈ 200
Type	Accessory | Back
Genres	Medieval
Description	Scorpio, the 8th sign of the zodiac, is symbolized by the enigmatic scorpion. You're sharp and strong, just like your sting.

Buy

Try On | 3D

☆ 1,697

ROBLOX

Astronaut Animation Pack
By ROBLOX

Price	Ⓡ 500
Type	Bundle
Description	This animation pack only works with R15 avatars. Boldly going where no Robloxian has gone before.

Buy

Astronaut Idle

☆ 643

WHERE TO FIND IT:
Avatar Animations, Bundles

NAME OF DEVELOPER:
ROBLOX

WHAT IT IS:
Astronaut Animation Pack

WHERE TO FIND IT:
Avatar Animations, Bundles

NAME OF DEVELOPER:
ROBLOX

WHAT IT IS:
Mage Animation Pack

Mage Animation Package
By ROBLOX

Price	Ⓡ 250
Type	Bundle
Description	This animation pack only works with R15 avatars. This guy is spellbinding - his magic show really put a spell on me!

Buy

Mage Run

☆ 1,850

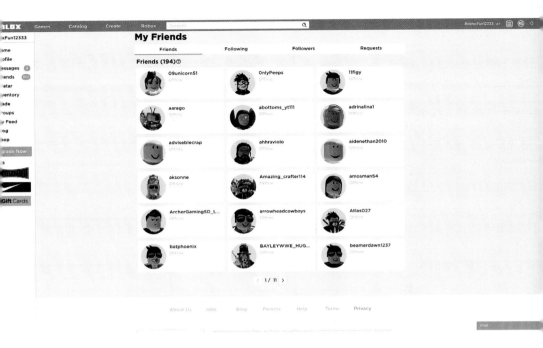

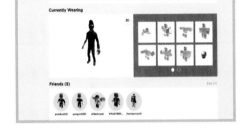

POPULAR AVATARS TO KNOW IN THE GAME

There are some avatars that truly stand out above the rest as impressive creations. These are the players that other Roblox visitors come to know and recognize. It's impressive when you come across these players in the game, and you'll remember them when you do.

Work really hard to create your own standout avatar and you can become part of the group of exclusive players who are known for having an awesome avatar! Better yet, you can create your own group of great looking avatars and all have fun together!

Here are some pictures of all the awesome figures we have seen so far this year! They're truly amazing to see in person and should help give you some ideas for your own creations!

ROBLOX

POPULAR AVATARS TO KNOW IN THE GAME GALLERY

Name: iEriin

Look: Black, purple and fun antlers to match!

Name: DrTrayblox

Look: This golden doctor is just as dapper as ever with a duck on his head and big glasses to match!

Name: iiGalactic_Ocean

Look: A little bit surprised, but with the ultimate arm and leg-piece to match. Stripes and denim complete the outfit.

Name: Aquamxrine

Look: Riding off into battle is easy to do when you have this awesome look. The sword, black emo look and awesome hair.

Name: Ninjalshu

Look: The face on this one is one that stands out. The awesome newspaper hat stands out and the black sweatshirt completes the look.

Name: kik12211

Look: This little avatar has funny skinny chicken legs, devil horns and a funny face which makes it stand out.

Name: Nataly5622

Look: This cool girl is a favorite character because of her backwards hat, awesome jeans and cool shirt.

Name: Jibrilmuhamad

Look: This avatar has an awesome stick, devil hat that stands out, devil wings, a peg leg and a cool mask that covers half his face.

ROBLOX

Name: Rodney_Roblox

Look: This golden guy is a majestic avatar that stands out, with gems and all on the crown. He surely is royal.

Name: alexnewton

Look: Red suits are in and complete with top hats, you know you're ready to check out all that comes from the game when dressed as good as this avatar.

Name: xxProRiko_Y

Look: Looking like he is ready for action, this avatar stands out with his awesome shades, gear on his back complete with weapon and awesome outfit.

Name: Herobrineplays210

Look: The awesome colorful lights around the avatar's head, the mask that gives it a scary look and the cool jacket make this avatar stand out.

Name: Rubystarman54

Look: Blue, black and fun all come together with this avatar that has a lot to show off. Complete with facemask and headphones, it really makes the look.

Name: Dgirl12343

Look: Antlers and a cool animal face is what really brings the look together. Black on black is what to expect with this outfit.

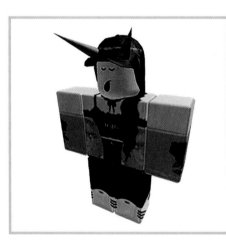

Name: Koalla_confetti

Look: This awesome outfit stands out but the horns on her head really complete the look. She looks bad and ready to take care of business.

Name: Puppyswag12233

Look: With a puppy coat and look you can expect the best look and feel that is wrapped on the outside of this avatar. The hat, the goggles, the hair and more are great.

ROBLOX

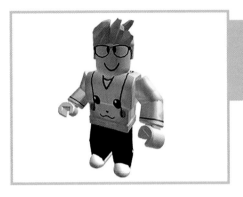

Name: Geekachu268

Look: If you have never seen a geekachu then you should know he is definitely wearing Pikachu, which is pretty awesome.

Name: coocoobirdco

Look: Another majestic avatar complete with awesome weapons, a great outfit and an ever better crown that stands out and sparkles.

Name: cardmaster395

Look: Pizza over the face is always an awesome look to have, but the top hat on this avatar is really what makes him stand out the most.

Name: girlhelpermom

Look: Purple hair and a more life-like face, this avatar is a beautiful one that really stands out from all those other block heads you see elsewhere.

Name: OnlyPeeps

Look: This avatar is covered in black and white and kind of looks like a mime, but that red hair and horns really makes it stand out from the others.

Name: batphoenix

Look: Purple and blue come together on this awesome avatar that looks like he runs with the cool kids crowd, are you his friend?

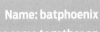

Name: camscool223

Look: His outfit is one of the best, not only is it cool and in style but the awesome friend he has on his shoulder is the cutest.

Name: adsonexpert101

Look: In addition to having an awesome name, this guy also has a unique look. He has an animal head, large awesome wings and a cool birthday cake hat.

ROBLOX

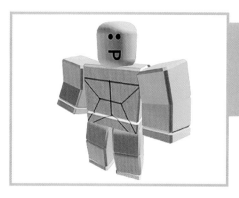

Name: EJGamer1122

Look: He kind of looks like a blue ninja turtle? Or maybe he used too much mint toothpaste, we are undecided but we do know he is too crazy cool to not mention.

Name: fluffi_taya15

Look: Who doesn't love rainbow hats and awesome looks? The smile on this avatar says it all and it is definitely one you're not going to forget.

Name: jul_apple012

Look: This avatar is one of the best just because of the fiery look in his eyes and the awesome gear he is wearing. Those robot parts are really going with the whole look.

Name: nexobaronpe24

Look: The fox hat on this character matched with the awesome red robe is different from many of the rest, plus you cannot even tell they have a block head like the rest of us, can you?

MEGA BUILDER

Name: Bubbahooligan

Look: What an awesome name! Not only that, but the hat you have on and the camera you're wearing makes you look like you're ready to capture all of Roblox's moments.

Name: GREENUNICORNDUH_3

Look: This avatar makes you believe they are a green unicorn, but they have a red mask on and black and white striped clothes. Pretty tricky we think.

Name: FuriousGamer11011YT

Look: Bright purple hair and an awesome ninja outfit is what he is able to bring to the table. What an awesome outfit that this avatar is wearing.

Name: galaxygamer0223

Look: Who says the boss can't have an animal face and wear some of the most colorful suits? This guy is doing it, so why can't you?

ROBLOX

Name: soysoyel

Look: This is probably one of the coolest avatars that I have come across. He has an awesome look and even awesomer face. If you're not playing games with this guy, you're going to want to be.

Name: Pugie_Derp123

Look: What? You were expecting something not so colorful? Think again. As one of the brightest and funnest avatars out there, you can find the rainbow is definitely with this avatar!

Name: Real_NickBrick02

Look: He might be small and look like doge, but he is mighty and able to take you down with his sword that is twice his body size. Awesome, different, deadly.

Name: primalfight

Look: His avatar is a cross between lizards and toads and majestic guitar players in some rock n roll bands we have never heard of. He is definitely quite the avatar to show off.

Currently Wearing

3D

Friends (30)

See All

| btss199roblox | getoutmywa... | cyber_kitty14 | cedrikmar | profyat0 | oneeyeowl32 | jomarieelnas | romeocanla... | tomandjerry... |

If you are the one that is playing the game, then you need to make sure that you're having fun with some of the items you can customize your avatar with.

With so many creative ways to change the outfits out and really make them shine, you can be different from every other avatar that might be playing in this game, which is a good thing if you don't want to be like the rest.

We can make sure you're seen in a sea full of players that might not have the awesome things you have.

Just throw them on and you can be sure to be seen!

Gain some inspiration from some of these awesome avatars and characters that you can say hi to when you find them in the game or come up with something that is completely your own and unique.

With so many items to choose from in the catalog, everyone is happier when they have something that appeals to them and their particular likes.

If you have your own fashion, then it might be time to show it off and really let others know how you look in real life, or perhaps, how you want to look in real life when you are customizing your avatar to be the one that stands out.

I am working on my look in the game, are you going to do the same?

We can customize and really get something together that makes us stand out as different until the next time we come around with a new book – who knows, your creation might be so awesome that you will be showcased in our next gallery feature section? ■

ap here to chat

1,000

0

ROBLOX

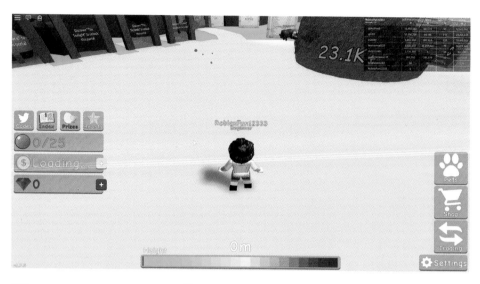

Popular Games to Play

Roblox is made up of millions of different games, which means that choosing the best ones can be tough. There are thousands of players making new games every day, and there are some pretty awesome creations available. By playing top games you'll enjoy top entertainment opportunities, and a chance to make some friends along the way as well.

Wondering which games you should play? Wondering what games are being offered from Roblox that you can play?

We put together this chapter with top-rated free play games. You can access any of these games for free, though some of them may have aspects, accessories, or extras that do require the player to pay to use them or put them into the account.

Check out these popular games that everyone else is playing and see for yourself what an awesome time you can have with them!

Pet Ranch Simulator

This opens up a whole new world that provides the player with a ranch that they can work on to earn money. You can then use the money to buy your pets things and raise them right, while also hatching new pets to raise on the ranch. There are over 40 different animals to choose from and you can have up to 50 on your own ranch. There are ultra-rare pets that can be hatched and collected.

Restaurant Tycoon

In this game you get to build and run your very own restaurant. You can serve a lot of customers and provide them delicious food items and collect the money. Build your restaurant with the money collected. You can grow the restaurant to much bigger sizes and take in more guests at the same time. Along the way you can add in music and other entertainment and additional enhancements to transform the atmosphere. Enjoy the thrills of restaurant ownership with this awesome game.

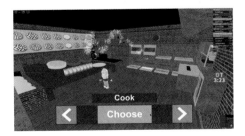

ROBLOX

Work at a Pizza Place

In this popular online game you're given a home to furnish and grow as you grow your pizza career. You work with a team to assemble the best pizza place that the neighborhood has ever had. With a store already made, you have to come up with a way to cook the pizzas, ring out the customers, deliver the pizza and more. You can choose which job you feel the most comfortable doing. Collect your paycheck and make the most of the house they give you in this game as you try and make it to the top.

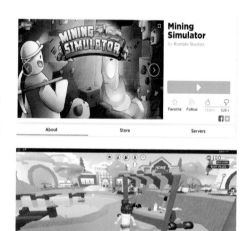

Mining Simulator

As a mining expert, you're tasked with climbing down into the depths and uncovering treasure. This is something that many of the players find intriguing because not only do you collect the money and gold that you dig out, but you can get so much more. You can look for rare gems that will ultimately make you a millionaire in the game. You can travel to different worlds to look through their mines and collect more. Get hats, pets and many other accessories to mine with in the game.

Cursed Islands

If you like to fight against strange and not-quite-human enemies, you have come to the right place. The cursed islands work to test your limits as you fight to remain alive. It is a survival game and if you have what it takes then you might make it off the island. It is exciting, well-built and one of the most popular games because of these aspects. If Cursed Islands sounds like a game for you, then enter into the world and start playing.

Robbery Simulator

Robbery Simulator has really thought of it all when it comes to living the life of a robber. It's up to you to find the most precious valuables and steal them for yourself, and then sell them off for some serious cash. Once you have some money you can buy disguises or even costumes that show off your robber level in the game. You can learn how to become stealthier and to avoid arrest again and again before the police ever show up. The game was recently updated and the police are harder than ever to outsmart. Do you have what it takes?

ROBLOX

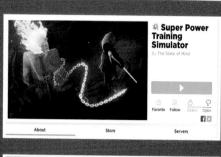

Super Power Training

Players that want big muscles and the powers of a real super hero can train in this simulator. The game provides everyone with everything they need to develop their super skills. If you want to rescue people or just punch through walls, you can do all of that and even more after a bit of training in this top Roblox game. Work hard enough and you'll become an invincible hero in this online game.

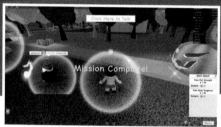

MeepCity

Become a part of a city that is growing and bustling with activity. You can find friends, get married, have children, get a job and do just about anything you can think of in this city. You get your very own estate that you're able to customize any way that you like with the cash you have available and the accessories and items you can purchase with it. There are badges to be won and players to talk to. This city is for everyone.

Theme Park Tycoon 2
By Den_S

Favorite · Follow · 533K+ · 52K+

About · Store · Servers

Weight Lifting Simulator 3
By Flamin' Studios

Favorite · Follow · 217K+ · 23K+

About · Store · Servers

Theme Park Tycoon

Everyone likes a good theme park, and now you can be the one that delivers it to them. Play Theme Park Tycoon and develop a park that you're proud of so you can show it off to the world. This is a game that you can play on your own or build with your friends. You're given a plot of land and you can build up from there. Add in roller coasters, extras, buildings, concessions and more. There are hundreds of pieces to choose from to make the park extra fun.

Weight Lifting Simulator

Want to become a body builder but don't feel like lifting weights for real? Now you can with the help of this simulator. Bench press, squat and overhead press your way to an impressive physique and try to become the toughest muscle head in this outdoor gym. The more you lift, the bigger your avatar is going to get. From the moment you start playing you can battle it out with the other players in the gym, making this online game into an entertaining combat simulator. Want the seat they're on? Want them to stop staring at you? Let them know and if they're a small fry, they might just get out of your way!

Creator Challenge

Do your best to build and create to complete the unique challenges in this Roblox game. Anyone that wants to try their luck and earn some badges to show off right from Roblox themselves can do so inside this game. You can work on different tasks that you are given and can complete different game goals over time. Creator Challenge is all about creating something awesome and unique. With everyone judging your builds depending on what the topic that is given, you can win the big prize or even runner up. See how many badges you can win with this one!

Murder Mystery 2

Who doesn't like a good mystery? When you go into this game, everyone is given a task or a job to accomplish. You might be the detective, the innocent people in the case, or the murderer in the game, you never know. It is a great mystery game that everyone can jump on board with.

Flee the Facility [Beta]
By A.W. Apps

Favorite Follow 705K+ 56K+

About   Store   Servers

Pet Simulator!
By BIG Games Simulators

Favorite Follow 527K+ 55K+

About   Store   Servers

Flee the Facility

Enter into an intense game of hide-and-seek for your life in Flee the Facility, the hit Roblox game. In this game you're tasked with hunting down the other players, or escaping from the beast with your life. You are located inside a little cabin in the woods and you have to make sure to be the one that leaves the game before the beast gets you. With serene landscapes, you will have plenty of places to hide, but will you make it?

Pet Simulator!

Everyone loves pets and when it comes to the pets simulator, you're going to be in pet heaven. The more coins you have, the more items you can get for your pets. You can also use coins to purchase eggs that you can use to raise even more pets in the game. You work together with other players to build and get better items. There are even rare items worth collecting in the game if you can find them. Trade with other players if you like what they have and work to build a pet collection that you're proud of.

ROBLOX

Dragons' Life

This role playing game allows you to be any sort of dragon that you want to be. You can enjoy being a dragon adult, teen, child or even an egg! You can enjoy playing with others in this game and take living as a dragon to the next level. There are a lot of things to do, plenty of customizations to apply to your dragon, many places to take advantage of and so much more. If you love dragons, this is a well put together game that welcomes everyone to come in and have a good time.

Hide and Seek

If you love hiding and seeking, then you have come to the right place because you can experience the thrill of the well-known game right here in Roblox. When you play this game you get to choose whether you want to hide or be the seeker. Once you've decided you're paired up with other players so you can enjoy the game exactly the way you want to. Start playing now and get hiding or seeking out the other players in the game.

Dungeon Quest

Do you like going on quests? Dungeon Quest is the ultimate test for you to enjoy as you try to run through the different obstacles. You'll battle a bunch of bots as you move through the levels and try to take the right paths. Do your best to choose every turn right and find your way out alive. Beat big bosses, bring your friends and so much more. Everyone else is ready for the unique challenge that Dungeon Quest offers. Are you? If dark dungeons filled with mystery and fun are your thing, then now is the time to check it out for yourself to see what's hidden within.

Zombie Attack

Everyone loves zombies and Zombie Attack gives you new and exciting ways to interact with these creatures. In the game you can either put them to work for you, or you're tasked with running away from them as you try to survive. You can collect zombies of your own, battle against bosses and work to make your army stronger and more exciting, or you can fight back against the zombies and try to survive. Whatever you do, work hard to get to the top and you could reach the number one position on the leader board!

ROBLOX

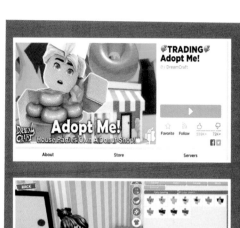

Adopt Me!

This trading game gives you the ability to collect some of the rarest items that you have ever seen. You can adopt or get adopted in the game depending on the person you choose. You can make a family, decorate a house and even trade items. The options are endless and the city you live in has everything that you need to call this game home. Bring some friends and play with them or make some new ones.

Ninja Masters

Who doesn't love to be a ninja? When it comes to being the master of the ninjas, this is the game for you. You grow your own ninja and can battle the other ninjas that you come across. When you grow stronger, your enemies are going to become stronger. Perfect your skills and see how far you can get going against some of the best players in the game in this popular Roblox title.

McDonald's Tycoon

If you enjoy McDonald's and you want to be the one in charge of creating a successful business, then this is the game that is going to welcome you inside to flip those burgers and serve those guests. The building provides the person with a way to play any of the positions that they want to play, and multiple players are able to play and run a McDonald's together. This is one of the most sought-after games that Roblox players enjoy today.

Roblox High School 2

Roblox High School is one of the best places for you to spend your time. With a new school for players to roam and check out on their own, you can become a part of the school. Make new friends, go to your classes, customize your avatar with new accessories, outfits and more.

ROBLOX

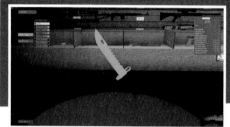

Prison Life

Choose whether you want to be a guard or a prisoner and start playing this hit Roblox game. work to contain the prisoners attempting to escape as one of the guards, or fight hard to gain your freedom as a trapped prisoner. There's so much to do in this online game that there's something to keep everyone busy as they play. Everyone is able to do multiple tasks while they are in this game, which makes it quite fun. The updates to the game added new accessories, features and weapons to use.

Epic Minigames

Epic Mini Games is actually a collection of many different games together to help keep you entertained and trying new experiences time and time again. There are 84 different games to choose from when you want to try something different, you can skip between the different games offered to find the one that speaks to you. There are even things you can collect while playing the mini games and you can unlock some pretty cool items if you spend time with the game.

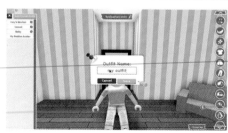

Treasure Hunt Simulator

Hunting for treasure is always an enjoyable experience and something that you'll remember long after you're done. In Treasure Hunt Simulator you're tasked with searching for treasure. If you're the one to find it you'll unlock exciting prizes and you'll enjoy yourself even more. While searching for treasure in this game you can also collect unique and rare items, and even rebirths and coins. The game has everything you could ever want and need to cash out on. Follow the map to find out where the treasure is to see what is inside!

Bubble Gum Simulator

Collect bubble gum and pets in this simulator that welcomes one and all to come inside for a great time. You have access to many different types of pets to own and play around with and, you're easily able to swap from one animal type to another whenever you need to while playing the game. There are different colors and flavors of bubble gum to collect in this Roblox game. You're also located in the beach area, which is a great place to be on the boardwalk.

ROBLOX

Dragon Ball Z Final Stand

Learn how to play against the other characters of Dragon Ball Z in this fun game that offers you a chance to win. Whether you're Goku or Gohan, you can be sure that you're kicking butt in this high flying action game that offers a look into the Dragon Ball Z world. Perfect your combat skills, train hard and work your way toward the title of Super Saiyan where you can dominate the competition.

Vehicle Simulator

Drive around some of the nicest vehicles in Roblox while earning cash and saving for other prized vehicles in Vehicle Simulator. This online game is simple to play, and addicting as well. This racing game won't just help you earn money to purchase new cars, it will task you with racing in some of the toughest competitions so you can test out your new purchases to see if they're built to win. The world is open to everyone, so try it out for yourself.

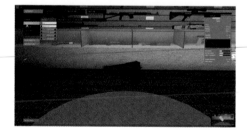

RoCitizens

This is a full-on world that everyone is welcome to come inside and join. You can work at jobs, build families, get a home and furnish it with awesome new upgraded furniture and items. You can cruise around the town in cars that are provided and more. This whole city is made with the players in mind. You can even customize your avatar to fit the particular role it plays and more.

Counter Blox

This is completely a fighting game. When you go in, you choose a team to be on. From there, you work to eliminate the other team in the game. You get your gear and weapons and head out into the map. It's your job to take out as many enemies as possible without being eliminated yourself. The more you take out from the team, the more money you get to upgrade the gear and weapons that you are able to use in the game. The maps are all ones that span across the entire globe, which is pretty cool because you get to see new worlds.

Now that you have an idea of what to expect from top games on Roblox, check out the ones that interest you the most. With a bit of searching you'll find the perfect place to spend your time or just some inspiration for creating your own world or game that others will love. Everyone can enjoy all the cool perks and features of Roblox once they find the perfect game for them. The game is full of diverse places as well, giving serious players even more to look forward to.

Whether you're making your own game or just want to see what others have come up with it makes a lot of sense to test out some of the featured games available on Roblox. You don't have to worry about not being able to find a game that appeals to you because there are so many options to choose from.

Which games are the ones that you like the most? Which games would you want to see showcased in another book? It is always good to have an idea of which ones you love and why! Plus, this awesome game offers everyone a chance to be creative in their own special way when creating a game all their own but being able to get ideas from others.

Start playing these popular games today!

ROBLOX

2019 Monthly Events

Roblox events are held all throughout the year, every year, for those that are a part of the game. These events are special to players that continue to get on the game because they offer a lot more than the game itself is able to. Events are exciting opportunities to walk away with some extra swag and rare collectible items.

Anyone that is interested in playing in any of these events are welcome to take part in them. Some of them are scheduled in advance, while others will come about seemingly randomly. You have to check the emails and announcements that Roblox makes to find out what is coming up for everyone in the Roblox community.

Events are a fun aspect of being part of the Roblox community, and definitely not something you want to miss out on!

What are the Events?

Events are specialized games and features that the game puts on specifically for interested players. These events usually have hidden treasures placed in different games throughout Roblox. They sometimes come with objectives and tasks for the person to do as well.

PIZZA PARTY

The special Roblox events have been going on for many years since the game has been going on. They are something that is loved by all players, and something gamers talk about long after they are over as well.

As mentioned previously by the makers of Roblox, when it comes to the scavenger hunts they are putting on, they want to incorporate more games that users have made into the events so that they can showcase their talents. This practice allows many more players to enjoy all that comes from what is being offered.

There are many opportunities that await you when you want to be a part of the hub and events that welcome the creative players to be a part of the fun that follows. When you enter your creative world into the event contest, you give yourself a chance at fame and you take full advantage of everything that these special events have to offer. Who knows, you could get picked and experience an amazing surge in visitor traffic as a result!

The events are ongoing and some of them are random, so make sure to keep an eye out for them over time. If you're interested in entering the next event, you should begin creating your own world right now so you'll be prepared. The sooner you enter, the better.

ROBLOX

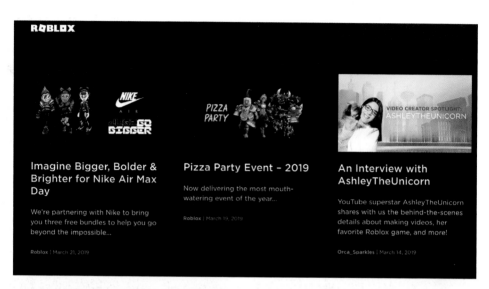

ROBLOX

Imagine Bigger, Bolder & Brighter for Nike Air Max Day

We're partnering with Nike to bring you three free bundles to help you go beyond the impossible...

Roblox | March 21, 2019

Pizza Party Event – 2019

Now delivering the most mouth-watering event of the year...

Roblox | March 19, 2019

An Interview with AshleyTheUnicorn

YouTube superstar AshleyTheUnicorn shares with us the behind-the-scenes details about making videos, her favorite Roblox game, and more!

Orca_Sparkles | March 14, 2019

Explore the Bloxys Theater to Earn Exclusive Prizes

February 12, 2019 by roblox

COMMUNITY   EVENTS

What You Do in the Events

The events all differ from one another, so the tasks that you have to do for each of them are going to vary. Keep this in mind as you approach each new event. Participants will receive instructions before the event starts. Roblox is known for giving shout outs and news announcements before a new event takes place, so pay attention and you'll always be prepared to enter and take part in the fun.

To get a general idea of what you can do in the events, here are some of the instructions and games that have been completed in the past.

Scavenger Hunts

Massive scale scavenger hunts are very common activities offered with many Roblox events. The makers hide a bunch of items throughout many different games. There are often up to 50 custom built games to visit in search of these special items. The players are told what the items are that they are hiding. Usually this is done around Easter, so they are eggs most often. Any players that want to take part in the celebration will have to search for the eggs or whatever has been hidden.

The 6th Annual

BLOXYS

Earn Exclusive Virtual Items

February 12th – March 5th

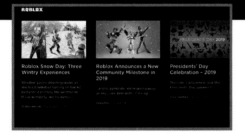

Roblox Snow Day: Three Wintry Experiences

Roblox Announces a New Community Milestone in 2019

Presidents' Day Celebration – 2019

This is one of the most well-known events that Roblox puts on and one that many people want to be a part of so they watch for it when that time of year rolls around. However, they also do different events for different holidays.

Players interested in being part of these events can find the applications right on the website. They fill these out and have to be 13 years of age in order to participate. Some of the selected worlds are paid and others are unpaid. The Roblox developers are who decides this when they accept the applications depending on the need of the world that is being entered.

Mini Goals and Objectives

Players looking for more objective-based games and experiences will love these types of special events in Roblox. For these events you are given quests to fulfill. Completing the different quests will grant you access to special rewards. Sometimes this is an item and other times it is a set amount of points. These points will add up giving you a chance to compete for the top position in the contest.

The Roblox developers mix in a variety of new and old games to keep everyone interested and to help celebrate games crafted throughout the years.

These events continue to provide extras that players need to thoroughly enjoy special occasions and to have a good time each time they log into Roblox.

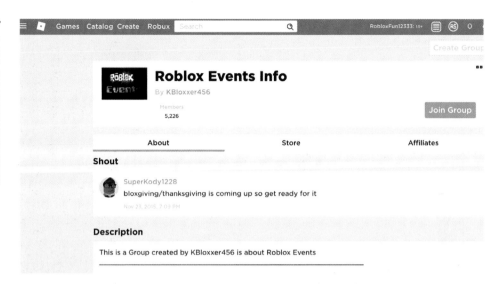

Roblox Events Info

By KBloxxer456

Members
5,226

Join Group

About　　　　Store　　　　Affiliates

Shout

SuperKody1228

bloxgiving/thanksgiving is coming up so get ready for it

Nov 23, 2015, 7:09 PM

Description

This is a Group created by KBloxxer456 is about Roblox Events

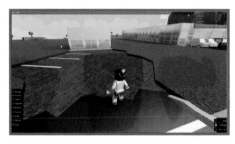

Calendar of Events

With so many exciting things happening around the world of Roblox, those that want to be a part of the games and mini games available can do so by using the calendar. This calendar lets you know every little thing that is happening from here on out. You can easily take part in the events that pique your interest as you browse through the calendar. You can even apply to have your world, game or avatar listed in many of the options that they are giving.

Some of the events are paid events and if you apply to showcase your work in them you can have an opportunity to get paid for using the game or world that you have in the event. This is one of the best reasons to apply, not only that, but seeing what you created being shown off is a great feeling and one you will remember for a long time.

Learn more about the upcoming events for the year, or the ones that have already passed. Even if you missed the events for the month, they continue to hold them every year, but try to make them better by improving off of feedback that players like you give them!

POWERS
EARN EXCLUSIVE PRIZES

January
Powers Event

In this special event players are tasked with locating their hidden powers and talents. During this special event many games are selected where you can find the tombs of untapped hidden energy to collect.

Additionally, those that are a part of the event can unlock added benefits by taking part in the special world event fights. It makes no difference if you're battling zombies or some other creature, you can win big from these battles. Try this special event out and enjoy a chance to unlock exclusive prizes! Battle, charge up, and make sure to get the best weapon to fight with!

Powers Event - 2019

January 17, 2019 by Roblox

COMMUNITY   EVENTS

A source of infinite energy can be found hidden deep inside the Roblox universe, but be wary, not all who seek this power aim to use it for good. Summon the courage from within and rally together with your fellow Robloxians to defend the catacombs from an invading mob, fight blood-thirsty zombies, and forge a legendary crystal sword to add to your strength. Show that the greatest power of all is your own and complete the following in-game quests by January 31st to earn exclusive prizes!

Swordburst 2

• **To Battle!** There's been an invasion at the Catacombs, and we can't afford to go back idly. Arm yourself with the strongest gear you can find, then head over there to fight against a horde of savage

The 6th Annual

BLOXYS

Earn Exclusive
Virtual Items

February 12th - March 5t

February

Bloxy Awards — Paid Event*

This event is held every year and it's an occasion that so many look forward to. After all, everyone likes receiving an award! Players that are a part of this event can watch big developers and players in the game get awards. Not only that, but players vote on who wins the awards, giving everyone something to do as the event unfolds.

Every player is welcome to become a part of this awesome ceremony and the past two years have been some of the biggest successes. Over 5,000,000 event prizes are given out to the players that find themselves being a part of this event.

March

Pizza Party

Take on the exciting task of creating your own pizza palace from scratch in this unique Roblox event. By joining in with the fun you'll have a chance to win you some big prizes and exclusive extras along the way. You just have to be prepared to get a lot of people coming and going from your pizza joint. They're also going to vote on whether or not it is one that makes the cut.

This is just an idea from last year. The Roblox developers might put a new twist on this and really make it stand out. It's a lot of fun to play creatively, and we're waiting to see what Roblox comes out with next year!

There will be pizza launchers during this event that you are not going to want to miss out on!

The Great Yolktales
Egg Hunt 2018

April

Scavenger Hunt – Egg Hunt – Paid Event*

One of the biggest events throughout the year, the egg hunt welcomes one and all to submit their worlds to become a part of the massive, site wide egg hunt event. With 50 or so games being a part of the event, the players that are not creating worlds or games for this event get to search around for the hidden eggs from all over the game world.

Players fortunate enough to find the eggs can cash them in for awesome prizes. The big egg hunt is one of the most loved events and one that is continuously being improved upon because it is the one that continues to stand strong even when some of the others are not doing so well.

ROBLOX

EVENT BREAKDOWN

7.1 MILLION
HOURS PLAYED

22 MILLION
VIRTUAL PRIZES EARNED

It is also a paid event, so players interested in submitting their worlds should fill out an application and hand it in to be considered. The organizers do request that the developer is 13 years of age or older.

Go on. Grab that gun. I dare you.

A mere two months after launch, <u>Murder Mystery</u> has amassed more than six million visits, a stunning accomplishment that has made it a fixture at the top of the ROBLOX game charts. In that time, it has only

May
Mystery

Mysteries are always exciting and if your game is selected as one of the games to take part in the event, then you can be sure that your world is being shown off. A lot of times, this is an event that challenges the makers to come up with a mystery game that holds the attention of the players and is fun for everyone. May the best maker win!

If you're interested in this one, sign up to be a part of it and to have your mystery game rated by the other players. You can win some pretty awesome stuff for taking part in the event.

Sponsored by **NEXT GEN**
A NETFLIX FILM
NETFLIX

June

Avatar

Decorating your avatar and dressing them up is one of the best aspects of Roblox and you've likely already done this at least a little. Did you know, they also put on an event that is dedicated to players that love to dress up their avatars? This means if you have a knack at making your guy or girl look stunning you might just have a chance at winning this exciting event opportunity.

Try on new outfits, make your own, build a world to show them off and more. There are many ways that this type of event can go, so make sure to look for official rules and guidelines on what exactly they request.

July

Racing

Who doesn't love a good race, or better yet creating your own racing games? If this is something you feel you're good at, then why not apply yourself and see if you can grab the award that comes with winning? Even the players that aren't responsible for creating new race tracks have a lot to enjoy about these events. That's because they get a chance to go up against one another in exciting races. Those that love to play the games also love it because they go through and rate the race courses for those that make them, so it is a win-win for everyone.

Racing is for everyone and when this event comes around, make sure you've brushed up on your track and car design skills so you can put together the best creation of them all.. You will find that this is one of the more exciting events that players enjoy, both raters and makers.

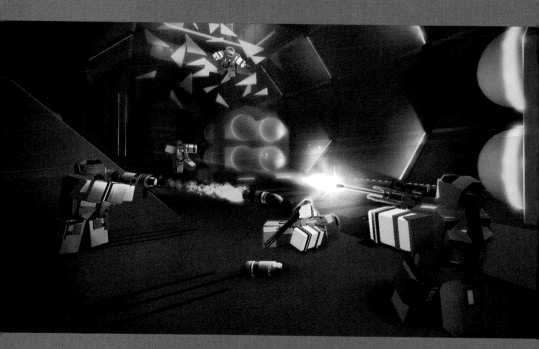

August

Back to School

Those that are going back to school will love being able to create their own classrooms and schools. In Back to School you get a chance to build a classroom from the ground up. That means you can be a part of a cool school creation. It's the perfect opportunity for creators to showcase their talent and to try and unlock some prizes at the same time.

We do want you to take part in the schools that are being built here, though. With multiple chances to win, consider what you would put inside your school and what other players might think is cool to see, have or do when they visit.

September

Fly Around the World – Paid Event*

Don't miss your chance to travel around the world and explore some of what it has to offer or to build part of a massive world and showcase your creative skills. In this special event you can create or explore to your heart's content. Whether you're making a piece of the world for the event or you're visiting the creations of others, there's something for everyone to love about this event. This big event is held annually, and a fun celebration of creativity in the Roblox universe.

This is another paid event and an exciting one at that. Don't miss your chance to build a world, or to fly around and explore and see the creative potential of so many makers in Roblox.

October

Future is Bright

The Future is Bright is one event that many are wondering about. Perhaps bringing the guests a futuristic world that only some of us are able to dream up or anything else you can think of. With so many ideas on this one, we will have to wait and see what the developers of Roblox are thinking of.

Of course, if you have some sweet rocket boots in mind to build, then this might be the perfect time to show them off to the world, so keep them in the back of your mind for when this event rolls around once again.

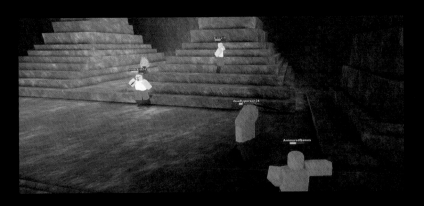

Did you know that your sword swings happens in sets of three, each blow doing more damage than the last? Pictured is the final of the three animations—the overhead blow—which does the most damage.

November

Royale

One of the biggest words on the street with this event is that there will be a Fortnite geared event that is going to drive everyone to really hunker down and make something happen. This is an event that many are looking forward to, especially since many want to make a Fortnite themed game in Roblox. With this special event you'll have a reason to try and design something related to Fortnite. It sounds like a lot of fun to us!

If this is something you're interested in, then watch for it before November because the rules and official sign ups will come out much sooner than that. If you're a big fan of Battle Royale in Fortnite, then now is your time to shine with this event!

December

Games of the Year

Games of the year is a fun event designed to celebrate the top games from throughout the year. There are multiple games of the year that you can expect to find in this event. Not only do they bring together some of the best games that players have come across, but the players out there that did not enter their games are able to vote on the games that made the cut. This allows those that like some of the games more than others to vote for them to win.

The games are then provided with a rating based on the players that have come to the games and tested them. This is a great event and a chance to see ways you can learn more and expand on your game-making knowledge that is needed in order to grow and become better.

See if your game can make the cut when you apply to become a part of the Games of the Year event that is offered.

It is also important to note that the explanations of the games are speculations. The developers of the games have just put out a heads up of what is coming without actually explaining them. With some speculation and observation from other players, the explanations are what might just happen and what you might want to prepare for if you are wanting to become a part of any of the events that are going to be held in the world of Roblox.

In all of the events that are being held, it is important to remember that the games have to be created from the ground up. In the past, those that wanted to be a part of the events could build onto the games that were already existing, but since then, the developers feel it would be more fair if every player in the event built the worlds from the ground up.

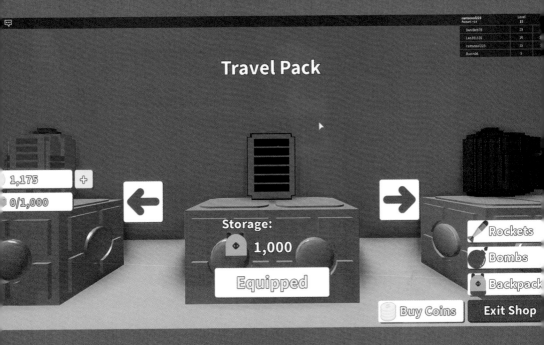

Travel Pack

1,175

0/1,000

Storage:
1,000

Equipped

Rockets

Bombs

Backpack

Buy Coins

Exit Shop

Want to know if playing in the events are worth the time you're putting in? Well, that depends on whether or not you enjoy the experience of each event, and if the items mean something to you or not.

There's no way to let you know if an event is worth it or not this year, because the items have not been offered up yet. This is usually a surprise, but they do provide rare and unique items for you to make use of so this is something to keep in mind when you're trying to grab the right items to put in your pockets.

These events are fun to play, and they definitely are a great way to spend your time on Roblox. When you want to enjoy playing with others or if you're competitive, they are a great way to get your creations out where others can see them.

Hidden Treasures to Know About in the Events

So, you want to know what types of hidden treasures are hidden in the events?

ROBLOX

Hidden Treasures in the Past Events

Many people talk about the many events that were available in the past and what they have gotten from being a part of them.

FREE ROBLOX MERCH!

This is one of the biggest wins that players that take part in the events get. You can get everything from free T-shirts to Robux that you can spend on the games you want to play or the categories that offer you fun stuff to use on your avatar from the catalog.

CASH PAYOUTS

Players that are a part of paid events can grab the cash that they want when they are voted as a top developer or creator for the game. This is one of the best things to think about when you are signing up to be a part of the game.

UNIQUE CATALOG PRIZES

Players that take part in the events and are chosen to showcase their worlds usually are given unique prizes that they are able to keep for their avatar. Those that are chosen to be a part of the events do not have to be winners in order to take advantage of the catalog pieces.

SHOWCASE THEIR TALENTS

Roblox players that want to showcase their talents and be shown on the front page of the games are given the ability to do so when you are chosen as a part of the event. This is one of the best things about being part of the many Roblox events, and often the main reason that creators take part.

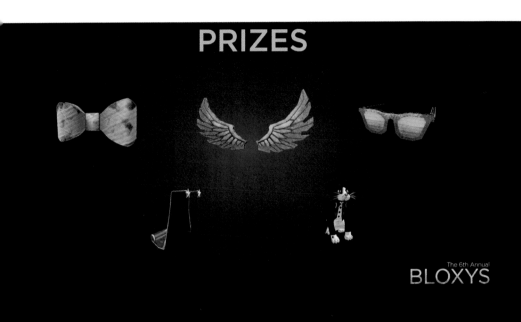

HIDDEN NEST EGGS

Those that are part of the scavenger hunt are able to find many hidden items that are put in the eggs that are hidden in the many different games during special events. These eggs are filled with items that you gather. The more eggs you gather, the more items and points you get. The person with the moist points that fulfill the treasure map are rated and can make it to the top of the list when they are put together.

Creating a game, even in the mini events that are being held, can get your creations viewed and noticed by so many. Release a top game and people all over Roblox are going to know about your creation, which is even more exciting than grabbing a few free items if you ask us.

Additionally, many of the mini games are given a theme, such as 'toys' that the game creators have to make a game or world based off of. If this sounds like a great time and way to build,

then now is the time to check out all that you can get from the events that are being offered from the Roblox game.

Now is the time to find out what you might do for the events that are coming around and which might be able to make you a winner in the end. After all, isn't that your main goal when playing events for any game out there? You join up with them hoping to be the main winner and to reap all the rewards.

Let the events begin and become a part of them today! Check the updates section for the next upcoming event to find out what you have to expect. The moment you hear about a new event is the time to submit your own creations for consideration. Work on your building skills and the next big event could be your time to shine!

Roblox makers love to have all their players take part in the events, so feel free to jump onboard! Creative caps on! ∎

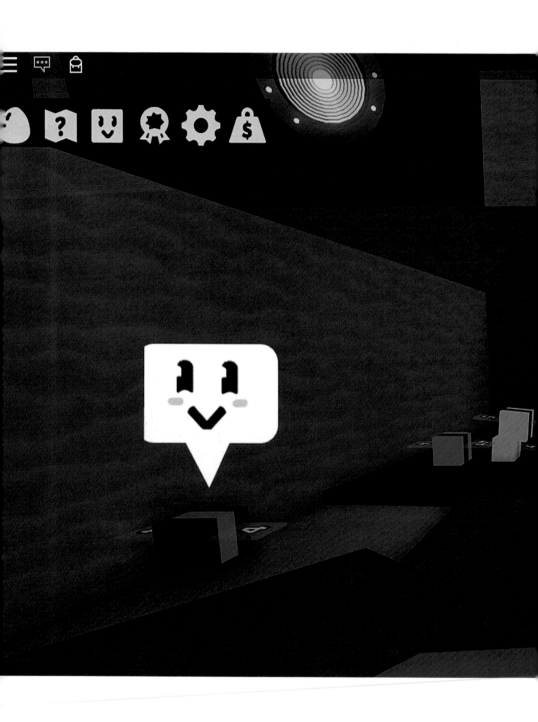

221/10000

Chat '/?' or '/help' for a list of chat comma

ROBLOX

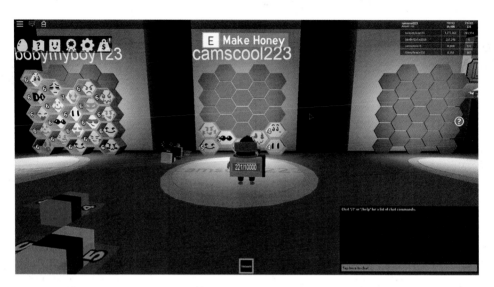

30,000 New Games Daily, Is Yours One of Them?

When it comes to unique and innovative games, Roblox is the place to find them. Countless new games are added to the platform every single day, giving you new options to try all the time. However, many of the old favorites remain on the front page which makes them easier than ever to find.

If you are looking at all of the new games that have been added by other players, then you are not going to want to miss some of these awesome finds. You'll always have a good time playing around with these top games, but you can use the excellent selection to give you new ideas for your own games as well. Use these game options to help you create something great of your own and give the rest of the community a game they can enjoy!

One of the best aspects of Roblox isn't the exciting games to play, but that feeling you get when you create a game of your own for others to try. However, you can't create something remarkable without first doing your research!

Make sure to play some games before you jump right into making them. You want to have an idea of what people like and what they want from games, and also what you enjoy in different games that you try.

Are you ready to see what awaits you when it comes to the new games, the top grossing games, the fun games and the games you can make on your own?

We are ready to take a look at all that is out there... are you?

New Games Recently Added

There are always new games recently added to Roblox. Every single day there are thousands of new additions! That means that you can play new games all the time, so feel free to check out the new additions and see what makes them stand out. Each one of the games we are showing here have great reviews from gamers that tested them out, even if they aren't the highest grossing or most popular games on Roblox just yet.

Take a look at each of our top picks and see if they have the fun that you are looking for and more. They might have exactly what you need to make them stand out and to help you have a good time. Even the unpopular games can offer something special, so don't be afraid to try them out as well!

Dinosaur Simulator

Want to know what it was like to live among the dinosaurs? This simulator gets you up close and personal with them. It is one pretty cool game and one that makes you feel like you are in the middle of Jurassic Park, which might be what you want. It's the perfect game for dinosaur fans, and it gives you a chance to explore and to take in the beauty that Roblox worlds have to offer.

Q-Clash

Ride into battle against other players to try to come out on top in this unique online battle game. Check out all of the classes that come up on the screen for you to play. You can try each one and ride into battle for a good time. When you play Q-Clash you get to be a character with specific powers, and it's up to you to do battle to the best of your abilities. What will you choose?

Horse World

If you love horses, then this is the world for you. There are tons of horses to care for to collect and to make into your own personal pets. You can choose which one you like the most and even breed and raise the ponies that come with them.

Dragon Ball Rage [UPD]
By iDracius

☆ Favorite   Follow   218K+ 👍   26K

About	Store	Servers

Description

Added 3 new forms, rescripted energy volley, and added custom ki color gamepass.

Dragon Ball Rage

Connect with the characters you know and love from the hit anime series in Dragon Ball Rage. The game is themed after the intense combat-filled series and opens up a world of exploration, battle and fun. Get on the game with your friends and battle against evil together or strive to become the toughest warrior on your world!

Feather Family [NEW COLORS]
By ShinyGriffin

Favorite Follow

About	Store	Servers

Description

Roleplay as a bird!

Feather Family

Ever wondered what it would be like to live as a bird? You'll have the opportunity to do just that in Feather Family. It puts you in the body of a bird and it's up to you to enjoy the freedom that being a bird affords you. As a bird, you are easily able to see everything happening below you on the ground. Soar high above and enjoy being a bird and flying free.

Arsenal
By ROLVe Community

Favorite Follow

About	Store	Servers

Description

https://devforum.roblox.com/t/arsenal-2-6-update/245788

Arsenal

You have to grab the golden knife and make a kill with the knife in the intense combat-based game Arsenal. Get your hands on the special knife and make as many kills as you can with it. That's the whole purpose of this online game. It is just that simple, or complicated, depending on how well you do.

ROBLOX

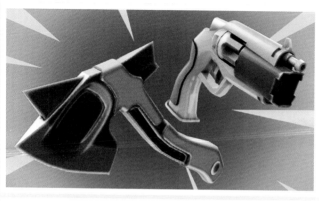

Murder
Mystery X
By Murder Mystery Prestiges

☆ Favorite 📶 Follow 👍 138K+ 👎 27K+

About | Store | Servers

Description

Start your adventure in the ultimate Murder Mystery game today! Deceive others as a murderer, save the

Murder Mystery X

If you love a good murder mystery, then this is the game for you. From the moment you begin playing this intriguing game it's up to you to figure out who committed the murder. You could even be the murderer, how's that for a plot twist?

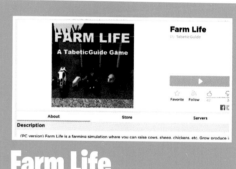

Farm Life
By TabeticGuide

☆ Favorite Follow 👍 42 👎 3

About | Store | Servers

Description

(PC version) Farm Life is a farming simulation where you can raise cows, sheep, chickens, etc. Grow produce i

Farm Life

Build and care for your very own farm in Farm Life. In this online game you get to grow a farm as large as you like and enjoy the benefits that come with being a farmer. It's up to you to care for all your plants and animals, and you could end up growing trees, vegetables, fruit, raising animals and more in this online game.

Mad City 🏙️
PYRAMID
HEIST 🏙️
By Schwifty Studios

☆ Favorite Follow 👍 336K+ 👎 112K+

About | Store | Servers

Description

Welcome to Mad City where the choice is yours to choose the power of good or evil. Cause chaos in the city streets as a criminal and super villain or join the super heroes and police force to bring justice to the city. With so many heists, the chaos never stops!

Mad City

Mad City gives you a whole city to rule over, which is perfect for anyone that likes being in control! You can join the band of villains that are running throughout the city or you can be one of the heroes that helps to protect the city. Whatever you choose, you are sure to have a good time while doing so.

YouTuber Tycoon
By #YouTube

☆ Favorite   🔊 Follow   👍 48K+   👎 53K+

About	Store	Servers

Description

Subscribe to Hiddo on YouTube for a 10.000 Cash Code:

YouTuber Tycoon

Work to become the most famous YouTuber in YouTuber Tycoon. In this game you need to use a series of machines in order to create a successful YouTube career. As you add in more machines, build up your views and generate new fans you could eventually become a famous YouTuber!

[UFO] Cursed Islands
By Sevon Levels

About	Store	Servers

Description
Lead, Scripted & UI Design by illusive

Cursed Islands

Battle your way across these islands though hordes of zombie enemies as you try and discover all the secrets the islands have to offer you. When you want something exciting and you like zombies, then this is the game for you to spend time on. You can discover more about the island when you take some time to explore them. Just make sure to bring a weapon so you can defend yourself.

Treasure Hunt Simulator
By HenryDev

About	Store	Servers

Description
Update 2.69 3/14 (VOLCANO UPDATE)
- Volcano (Main > Volcano)

Treasure Hunt Simulator

Search around for buried treasure and try to become rich and famous at the same time in Treasure Hunt Simulator. In this online game you'll be digging in different locations, tracking down rare valuables and making some pretty cool friends that you'll want to play with again and again.

ROBLOX

2 Player Superhero Tycoon

By santos_1121

☆ Favorite 📶 Follow 👍 109 👎 346

About   Store   Servers

Description

Team up with a friend to build your tycoon and eliminate enemy teams. Fight bosses to get diamonds that you

2 Player Superhero Tycoon

Superhero games are a lot of fun, because they let you step into the life of a real hero. 2 Player Superhero Tycoon is something special though. It has you work alongside another player to create a powerful pair of superheroes that you two can enjoy together. Partner up with a friend and become the most powerful heroes in the whole game world through this action-packed game.

After The Flash: Mirage
By After The Flash Advisory Board

☆ Favorite Follow 👍 28K+ 👎 2,930

About   Store   Servers
Description
Nothing's been the same since 2032.

After the Flash: Mirage

Those old western tales have nothing on this one. Except it is set in the future where the world has been wiped out and now you have to survive the hardships of being one of the ones left behind. It's a fun game based on survival and exploration and challenges you to think of new ways to survive as you try to live in this desolate landscape.

Water park
By Brer_Bear

☆ Favorite Follow 👍 5.8K+ 👎 12M+

About   Store   Servers
Description
Welcome to the water park!
This is one of the first games that I created on Roblox, which is why it might look and feel a bit outdated.

Water Park

Everyone likes a good water slide and when you are a part of this game, you can play in the pools, in the parks and on the slides that follow. You and everyone else in the world will have a great time playing on all the different attractions in your very own park. The water park wins a big vote on a great game to visit.

Scuba Diving at Quill Lake
By ColonelGraff

Favorite   Follow   156K+   13K+

About   Store   Servers

Description

Thanks for playing! Check out my ALL NEW Western game out in beta now!

Scuba Diving at Quill Lake

If you are looking at taking a dip, then you have come to the right place. Dive down under the surface and take a look at all the fish and underwater life that awaits you. It's a beautiful game that offers captivating scenery. Of course, there are also some dangerous things that are hiding under the waters.

Natural Disaster Survival

Want to survive the natural disaster that just blew through this world? You can enter and be a part of history in the making for the next Robloxians to rebuild. Find out the hardships that await and the fun to be had in this game that offers a bit of everything, including excitement.

ROBLOX

Monsters of Etheria

Part of the pizza party event, this is one game that is always updated and provides a lot of fun. You just have to help run the shop and make sure that everyone gets served in the right amount time.

Afton's Family Diner

Want to visit a diner and spend time getting to know some great people while having delicious food along the way? That's exactly what you'll do in this unique game. You can either work behind the counters, serve up the food or be a visitor that is there to enjoy a good meal. The choice is yours, but everyone is welcome in the diner that brings one and all together!

Pizza Factory Tycoon

Work hard to develop your own pizza factory in this one-of-a-kind tycoon game. Sure, it operates like all the other tycoons, but you get to experience the excitement of running your own pizza shop as you play. You don't have to worry about serving up those pizzas so quickly because you'll be more focused on decisions that help your pizza shop run well over the long-term. but being able to have fun running a pizza shop is a good thing and you can learn something from this.

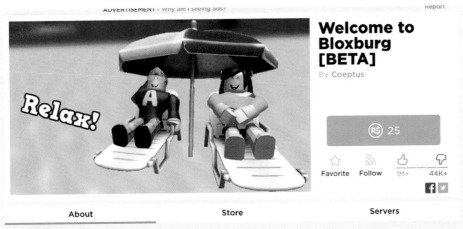

Top Earning Games

There are many top grossing games on Roblox and often times the top grossing games are also the most fun to play around with. It's up to you to make sure you're testing them out and that you find the options that you like the best overall. Not only that, but you can pick up some tricks and tips from these games that are winning big time that you can incorporate into your own creations.

Test out as many of these top-grossing games on Roblox as you can. They're sure to afford you an unforgettable experience and will likely inspire you to create a top-performing game of your own as well!

Welcome to Bloxburg

Everyone loves Bloxburg, it's a game that lets you have a family, buy a house and live an ordinary everyday life. It's a lot of fun to build up your character and to become an active part of the community as well. Make sure you give this online game your all, because when you try really hard to play this game that's when you have the most fun! Get together with a group of current friends and play or form brand-new friendships with this cool online game.

Royale High

One of the most favorited games out there, this is definitely one that offers a good mix of fun and excitement. You'll enjoy dressing up your characters and interacting with the other players on this world. Some of the items cost real money to access, but you don't need to use them and there's plenty of fun to be had for all.

ROBLOX

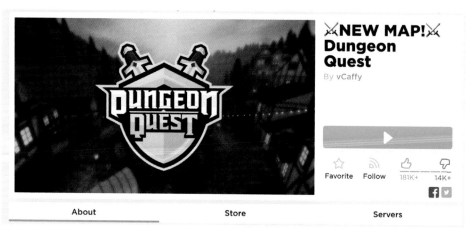

⚔NEW MAP!⚔
Dungeon Quest
By vCaffy

Favorite Follow 181K+ 14K+

About   Store   Servers

Dungeon Quest

Race through the dungeons and try your luck at winning against many of the bosses you come across in Dungeon Quest. You could win treasure and other exciting rewards during your journeys. You can even upgrade your gear when you make it to certain points in the game.

Bubble Gum Simulator
By Rumble Studios

Favorite Follow 440K+ 42K+

About   Store   Servers

Description

Jailbreak 🚔
HELI BOMBS 🚔
By Badimo

Favorite Follow 2M+ 575K+

About   Store   Servers

Description

Jailbreak Military

When searching for the perfect game to be the bad guy or the good guy in, Jailbreak Military is the ultimate option to consider. You can try to escape, or you can be the one trying to catch those escaping from the area. The choice is yours.

Bubble Gum Simulator

If you love everything about bubble gum, then this is the simulator just for you. You just have to walk into the simulator, and you're given gum, a nice relaxing place to chew it and can enjoy everything that comes with chewing bubble gum. It's a simple game, but surprisingly entertaining.

[Juuzou Trainer!] Ro-Ghoul [ALPHA]

By SushiWalrus

☆ Favorite   🔊 Follow   👍 218K+   👎 32K+

About   Store   Servers

Description

Ro-Ghoul

This is an Alpha game, but it is one that is doing awesome. They give you masks that you can use and even a Scorpion. So, if you are looking for a great time then this is the battle game for you. Fight for your Mortal Combat soul and have some fun while doing battle with your fellow players.

Mansion Tycoon

Ever wanted to know what it is like to live in a mansion for the summer? This game allows you to build on, to throw parties and to have the ultimate summer with the use of this tycoon game. Top grossing and definitely one of the more popular options.

ROBLOX

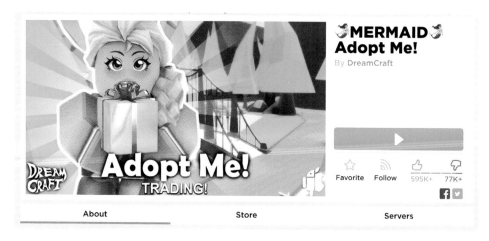

Adopt Me!

You can be the parents, the baby or someone else in this game. With new items always being added, you can purchase all of the baby items you need to take care of the baby you just adopted. You can even design your home and make a family with all of the other players in the game.

Vehicle Simulator

Ever wanted to know what it was like to drive around in a vehicle? We have the answers you are after. In this exciting game, you can jump in the vehicle of your dreams and drive around town. The sky is your limit here. Drive to earn more money that you can use to purchase more expensive and exciting vehicles in this cool driving game.

Phantom Forces

This is a shooting game that requires strategy and skill to win. While playing this game it is up to you to run around the map, hide and fight your way to victory. This can be done with the use of the guns and ammo that you find hiding around. It is exciting and you can keep advancing to the next stage when you beat the current one you are on.

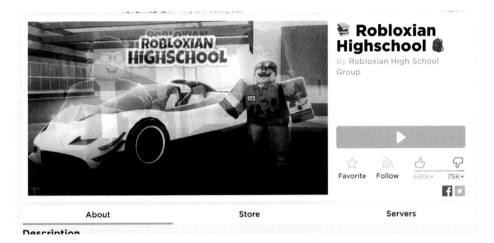

Robloxian Highschool

If you want to be in highschool, then this is the highschool to be in. Which group of kids do you run with? Who do you fit in with? Are you going to be a popular kid in school? You can have all of the answers and more when you play Robloxian Highschool. Make friends and do your studies and you'll go places in this game.

Bee Swarm Simulator

Ever wondered what it would feel like to have bees swarming you? This game actually gives you a chance to take care of them. You'll meet friendly bears and more in this fun game that lets you get a bit closer than you'd normally be able to get. Being a bee keeper can be fun.

MeepCity

This is one of the games that so many people hear about when they go to play Roblox. It is a very popular game and it is also one of the games that is currently making the most money. Start by customizing your own character and you can start enjoying all that this game has to offer you.

ROBLOX

Baby Simulator

This simulator works like the others and when you want to be a baby and forget about everything else you have to do in the real world, this is the game to play. The game has a bunch of toys, and additional special features that help to keep it interesting over time.

These games all have one thing in common – they are making top dollars! They are some of the most popular and highest earning games in all of Roblox, and they're the ones that you want to try out to see what Roblox has to offer.

If you think you have what it takes to make a game like this then we definitely invite you to try. It will take serious skill and creativity to make a game that players flock to, but once you do you'll find it easier to make successful games in the future, and you could become the next hit creator! If you can make it on this competitive Roblox platform, the sky is the limit to what else you can accomplish in your life.

Start thinking, because now is your time to shine and create a game that you and others love to play, are you ready to start building?

Making Your Own Top Played Game
Want to make your own top played game?

We put together some great tips and tricks for you to use in the other chapters and even a quick start guide on coding and building in the game. You can find just about everything that you need to monetize the game once you get it put together.

The biggest and best advice you can get about creating your own game is that you should definitely take a look around and play the games that others are playing. You want to make sure that you're offering similar themes and features that players clearly enjoy in Roblox. This is the most effective way to get ideas for your own games.

Even if you have some pretty good ideas, make sure that you're doing your research. Take the time to test out some of the top games on Roblox. That's a good thing anyway, I mean who doesn't love to play games on Roblox!

We know we do!

Building a game is almost like building with virtual Legos online. You get to build the look and feel that you want. You also get to control exactly how your game behaves through careful coding with Lua.

ROBLOX

You want to create your own things within the game because this is what makes it more popular. When you create objects from scratch players are more excited because they are getting something, new, unique, and fresh which is awesome. From the moment they get into your game they will notice it isn't like anyone else's on Roblox, and that's what will make it a top pick! This means that you don't want to overuse the free characters that are given to you while creating your final world. It's okay to use the free objects when you're just starting out and learning how to build though!

Always make sure that you test out the place that you make. When you do this, you're allowing yourself to have the time needed to fix any problems your game has. A great way to test out your world is to invite some of your friends into your game to try it out as well. This gives you a fresh set of eyes and you can listen to their recommendations once they go through the game.

You can even let the people in the game earn badges when they become a part of it. This means they work towards something while they are a part of the game, which brings in more players to try and earn their way to the winning end of the game.

Want to know the top games that players have made that really make money?

Want to make one of these types of games on your own and see how well they can do?

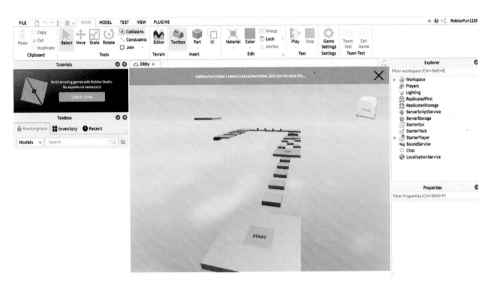

You just have to remember to put your own twist on the game and give it a theme that no one else has used previously. Do that while creating an enjoyable game and you might just have something that actually sells! If there is another one out there just like it, no one is going to want to visit both of them, unless yours is much, much better.

The Obby

Everyone loves a good obstacle course and with the use of this theme and template, you can create a pretty awesome one using the bits and pieces that are given to you for free. The obby is an exciting obstacle course that packs in unique challenges and gives players something to work toward that will make them want to keep coming back for more.

You can create a survival twist to this, you can add extras in around every corner, you can hide things and more. There are so many ideas and uses you can make use of when you are making an obby for your Roblox game.

Tycoon

Unlike some of the other options out there, the tycoon template is pretty bland on what it looks like, which is why this is one of the games that you have to put a lot of thought and time into when you create it.

The best part though, is that they usually get a lot of people that come to them and want to play them. You just have to think of a really good tycoon idea. If you can think of an impressive idea, you'll want to show off and that others will want to play.

Racing Game

Want to race some pretty cool cars? In the Builder tool you can create exciting and intricate tracks and even add in custom vehicles to your world. Whether they are coming for some leisurely driving around the track or if you are looking for a way to race people, this is where you can find yourself going.

Create a race track that will be the ultimate in racing fun. If you create a good racing game in Roblox you have a chance to earn plenty of Robux. Invite your friends over to your world to test it out before you finalize the game, and release something special into the community.

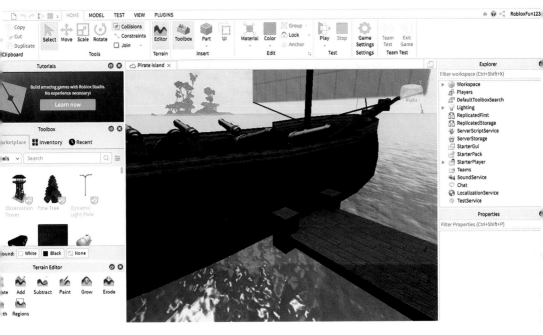

Adventure Game

Creating an Adventure Game is a chance to take your players on a unique adventure through a world that you created. In your game you get to choose an adventure template and then create a unique theme and design for your game. To make your game stand out give it a unique story and design that is different from the rest and work hard to make sure all the features of your game work properly.

Take your time and brainstorm some ideas for creating the best adventure game that is going to be able to get the job done. You want something that allows you to have a good time and adventure games are definitely where it's at.

There is always room for improvement, regardless of what you have made or how much time you have put into the game. This is true for anything that you create. When you want to make a top selling game, it is definitely going to be trial and error, because you don't know what exactly is going to work for the people that come and play.

ROBLOX

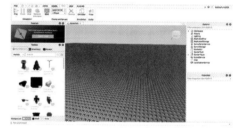

If you're ready to create a game that is going to really sell and that players are going to love, then you have come to the right place. You need to take the time to research the competition by playing top-rated games and highly popular games. Then you need to take the features that stand out from those games and work them into your own, or at the very least create your game with the same level of quality that the other people are offering.

Create at that high level and you'll enjoy more success and more earnings from Roblox as well.

Take a second to write down some ideas and then expand on those that you like the most. From there, you might be able to find the best played game on Roblox once you take some time to learn some coding and how to use the Roblox designer software.

Being able to make something that sells is not as hard as it seems. You are easily able to take some time to learn more about it on the side. If you are creative, you have a huge advantage on your side. Anyone can create a game, but you are able to create one of the BEST games out there!

With so many games being offered, it's up to you to find the one that you like to play the most. This is important when you want to spend time enjoying the life of a master player and a master creator in Roblox.

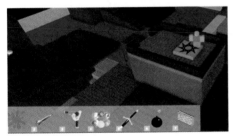

Everyone is welcome to play and create on Roblox, and that's what makes the game so special.

If you are looking for a game that lets you do so much and lets you be the one in charge of what you do and when you do it, then Roblox is the game for you. Every single time you sign on you can have a good time.

If you want to try creating a game, you're free to do so without ever showing the world. Create a practice game, play around with it, improve it and eventually release your game to the world, or keep it private forever for you and your friends to enjoy.

Check out the latest, the greatest and the other games being offered today to see which ones you like and which you might want to build when you go to make a game that everyone loves.

If you love that type of game, then make one.

Put a twist on it, make it your own and enjoy every minute of being a part of something awesome!

ROBLOX

VIP

x1.5 Bucks Per Round,
VIP Chat tag,
Rainbow Chat Color,
2 VIP only characters,
VIP Only Kill Effect,
One time +1400 Bucks

PURCHASE

Inspiring Imagination with Roblox Games

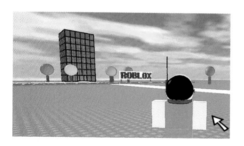

Roblox has been around for years and years, and over that time so many things have changed and evolved. The game was created in 2004 and released in 2006 and because of that the creators have had many years to grow the game and make it much more successful than it was in the beginning. This success continues to grow every day because of players (LIKE YOU!) that make this possible.

Roblox didn't just create the main website with a solid platform for gamers to have fun on online, but also encouraged players to participate, to be creative and to make new and exciting improvements to the game.

How?

When Roblox welcomed the use of the website, they welcomed players to come in and create new games on their own. These new games are meant to inspire and grow with the game and the website.

As a developer on the website, you can build just about any game imaginable. The builder is designed to let anyone enhance the website and create something for the benefit of other Roblox players.

A screenshot from Egg Hunt: The Great Yolktales (2018). Roblox sure has changed a lot since 2006!

A little-known fact is that Roblox has been out for many, many years and didn't become big until very recently. It became extremely popular after a base of kids discovered the game and spread information about it everywhere they could online. This helped to grow the website. Not only that, players on YouTube served as a promotional springboard that really helped push the game to be the ultra-successful game that it is today.

So what else does Roblox have to offer and what has it given throughout the years that you may (or may not have) been around for...

The Big Roblox Logo Change

When Roblox decided to change their logo, so many people were baffled by the change and design that they didn't know what to do. While this wasn't the only change that Roblox made, it was definitely one that caught a lot of attention.

ROBLOX

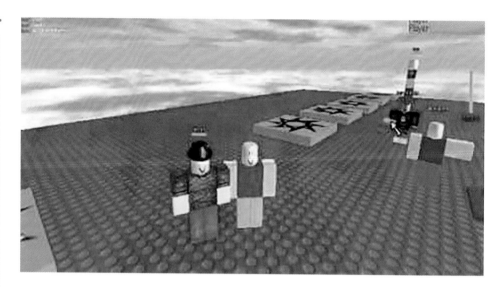

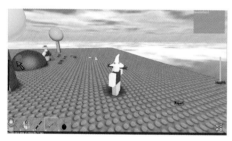

Roblox Sparking Imaginations in Kids

Roblox is well-known for its ability to inspire children to imagine and to push them to show off their creativity and design skills. Each visit to Roblox is a chance to witness some of the new creations put together by kids from all over the country. While Roblox has definitely made some of the games themselves, they also leave a lot of slots open for players that want to flex their creative muscles. The more popular the game gets that players make, the more people are going to be able to see it because it is pushed towards the front of the website for one and all to visit. This results in ultra-successful and popular creators that are able to have repeat successes on the Roblox platform.

The best part about this game is that it brings everyone together and creates the best platform to create and share worlds and games on.

Most players didn't know anything about an upcoming logo change, and this caught players off guard after it happened. While this didn't change the way the game was played or how it functioned, it still made people uncomfortable at first. Now, it is the logo that sticks with the game and the one that everyone now knows is associated with Roblox.

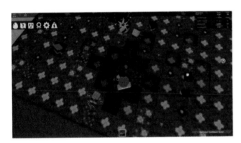

The main goal for the game is to create an alternate universe where everyone is able to spend some time creating some of the best games and worlds. The developers work really hard to make sure Roblox remains the sort of game that continues to encourage creativity and to generate some excellent online games to play around with.

Do you know what changes have been made in the game recently? How about the changes that have been made in the game from when it first came out?

Changes Made to Roblox Over the Years

There have been many changes made to Roblox over the years and due to the changes, a lot of people are wondering what else can be changed?

Roblox recently transformed the blocky and cartoony avatars into more realistic characters that look like real people. This is the newest and by far one of the best changes that Roblox has made to the players. Many people are in love with the new avatars and the change brought in a whole new group of players to Roblox.

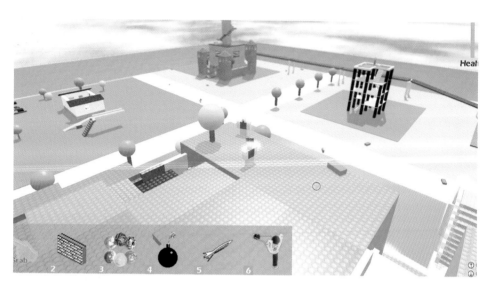

Heal

2006-2011 Back To The Past! [Game-Teleports]
Preloading Assets

AVATAR CHANGES

In the years past, the avatars were much blockier. They had sharp edges and were able to provide the user with a person, but the person was harder to customize and personalize, unlike they are now. Currently, the avatars that the players can choose from are rounded out and they have more lifelike appearances and shapes.

ROBLOX CREATOR

Roblox also made some pretty significant changes to their building system. They added more and more stuff throughout the years to make creating easier for developers. This is especially true for the kids that want to have fun creating and still make something worth playing with.

The creator is now so user friendly that even the youngest of players is able to go on the game and make their own world or create a game to put out there for other players.

The Premium Items

There has been a change to the premium items that are offered in the catalog. So many people now have more to choose from when shopping through the catalog, making it easier than ever to find an item that you love. Initially the catalog wasn't even a feature available to Roblox players. This changed recently, and it provides everyone with a way to customize and create their own avatar, so they can show off their own unique personality.

If you want to know more about this game, there is so much else that it has to offer. Roblox continues to change and will likely offer more exciting features in the future than what it has to show off today.

TICKETS TO ROBUX

While both existed in the very beginning, Robux stayed and tickets were something that the game got rid of. Tickets were used to cash in for new items and those items that not everyone had. These items would change out every month or so, so that none of the items were the same.

Tickets were used in Roblox from 2007 to 2016, so they have not been gone for that long, but long enough to where new players would not remember using them or even having them in their accounts at all.

MAKING THE GAME SAFER

The makers of the game heard parents and their pleas for help to make the game a bit safer for all to play, especially those that were under the

age of 13. The chat filter was then developed so that those that wanted to come on and play but needed safety nets in place were able to do so with the new filters.

While these are filters that some found annoying, they were able to cut out a lot of the stuff that younger kids were seeing or that were being presented to them. This also helped to reduce the number of kids that were going into games that were not age-appropriate.

ROBLOX

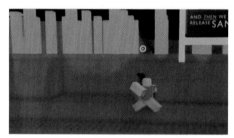

Those that go into the game and that are underage do require their parent's permission to play now. This is verified through your parent's email account, so if you don't yet have a Roblox account, make sure you get your parent's permission before you sign up! You're going to need their email to do so!

BETTER GRAPHICS, BETTER GAMEPLAY

One of the best things about the changes that have been made to Roblox is the graphics! Not only do the games and worlds that you put together seem nicer and clearer, but the graphics are some of the best.

In the beginning of the game's history, the graphics were blurry, and they did not show off a lot of anything. As time moved forward, the lines on the graphics have become clearer and they come together well to create an ultimate world or game for you to play.

Since the game relies a lot on graphics, this is an important upgrade or update for the website to go through.

Classic Roblox Coming Back at It

If you have never seen or played the classic version of Roblox, then you might feel like you are not missing out, but when it comes to playing something that has been around for so long, you want to make sure that you trace it back to its roots, so you can check out where everything came from. Strip away all of the extras and see what Roblox looked like in the beginning. If nothing else playing the classic mode will help you appreciate how far the game has come.

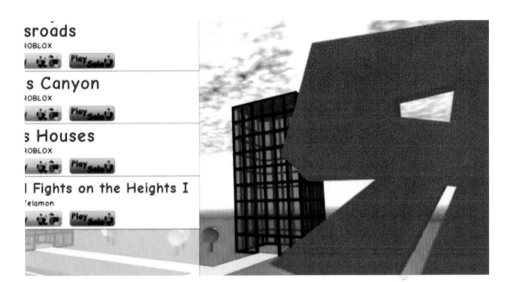

sroads
ROBLOX

s Canyon
ROBLOX

s Houses
ROBLOX

l Fights on the Heights I
Telamon

CLASSIC ROBLOX 1-4

Many big-name developers have released a classic version of their famous games later on. Nintendo is an excellent example of this with its Mario franchise, but there are others as well. Roblox is doing the same thing now, and if you've ever been curious about what the game had to offer when it got started years ago, test it out through Classic Mode and find out for yourself.

Roblox continues to grow and it will continue to grow as long as there are kids, like you, that continue to play. Due to this, it has not only went from a small online game to something that has its own large website, a creative building mode, many events and specialty items and so much more. Those that want to become a part of something bigger can sign up for Roblox and start creating their own worlds and games.

Take the time to look through the many games offered and find the one that fits the needs that you have. You want to take some time to enjoy playing on this platform because as times change and technology gets better, you will likely notice that Roblox will go right along and change with it.

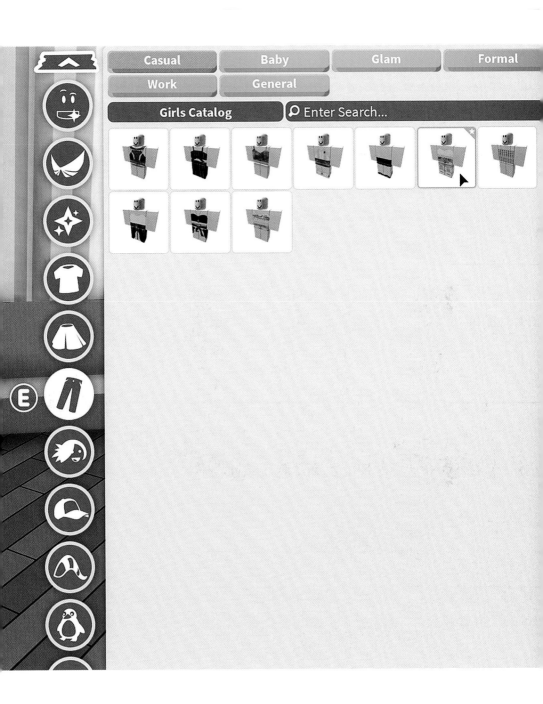

ROBLOX

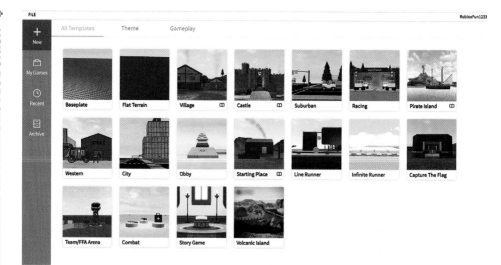

Using Roblox Studio to Create Your Own Games

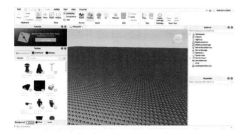

If you're trying to make your own awesome games in Roblox that actually sell, then having a quick-start tutorial to give you some direction, tips, tricks and ideas is going to be very helpful. By being able to have this information handy, you can create some of the best games out there.

The best part is that if you are a part of Builders Club, you don't have to settle for just one game. You can have a handful of them to try and offer to your friends. Just make sure to have a clear idea of what it is that you want to build and offer. It's important to know what is going to sell and what exactly is going to uplift those players that come in.

What will make them keep coming back for more? What do players like? What are some of the games that players go into often?

By knowing the answers to these questions, you can easily create a game that players will enjoy overall. This is a good thing to keep in mind because you don't want to just assume that they are going to be into what you are into.

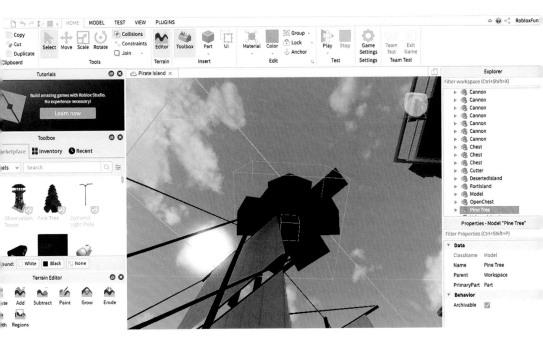

Once you do some research on the games out there as well as the players and have an idea of what you want to play, make sure to use this quick-start guide to your advantage. With a bit of our help you can really create a game that other players are going to want to check out.

Game on!

OVERVIEW OF ROBLOX STUDIO

Roblox Studio is a powerful tool that helps players build and create games and world of their own. If you can think it up, you're easily able to make it happen in the world that you get on Roblox. That was something that the creators of the game wanted to make sure that players were able to do.

As they continued to develop the game, this was something that ended up getting better and better with time. Using Lua, the programming language that is easy, colorful and provides endless abilities, many players, even the youngest of players, are able to make and code their own games throughout the Roblox world.

ROBLOX

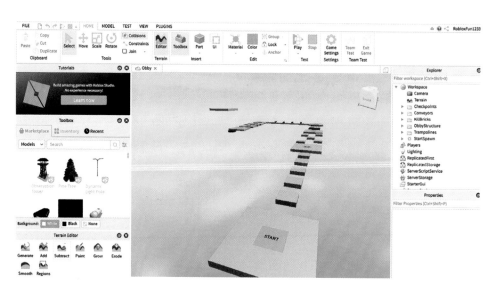

The best part about knowing Lua?

When you create the game that everyone wants to play, you can potentially make thousands of dollars if it becomes popular enough to all the gamers that get on Roblox. With a more popular game, you're going to get players coming from all over. They will pay money to go into your game, pay money for the items inside the game, or pay for whatever you have set up in the game for them to pay.

The Studio is easily opened, just like the game, but the diamond is a blue one instead of a red one. It provides the user with a way to develop their coding and building skills online and is easy to use.

Once you open the program, it invites you go through a tutorial. If you need more guidance, then this is something to definitely walk through and to use as a learning aid. You need to make sure you're obtaining all the building tips and information available, and the tutorial is an excellent place to start.

We invite you to learn more about Lua and what others are saying about the program online. Having some information on this programming language is great when you want to make more advanced things happen in your games. We will give you some insight here, but you'll want to look through the tutorial and to play around with the language itself to really perfect your programming skills.

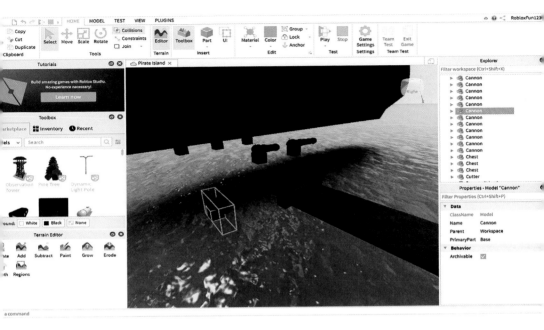

HOW TO USE ALL OF THE ROBLOX STUDIO TOOLS

There are many different tools for players that help to create games in Roblox Studio. Here is a quick breakdown of what you can use when it comes to the Roblox Studio tools and the different tabs. Once the player is familiar with the different tools, they will have all they need to create exciting games.

There so many tools at the top of the Roblox Studio. When you choose your theme or template and you start to make your game, then you should have a decent idea of how to start, which tools will work best for you and how to create your idea.

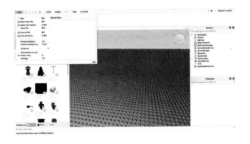

Item Bar

On the left of the screen, there are items that you can add to your game. You just have to click on this to pull them and place them in the game.

Analyze

This section is the Physics Analyzer. This is a very useful tool. When the game is being played, you can go through and continue to play it without worrying about what is wrong. The analyzer will let you know what issues are occurring underneath the surface and give you ideas about how to resolve your problems.

Screenshots: Roblox® ™ & © 2019 Roblox Corporation

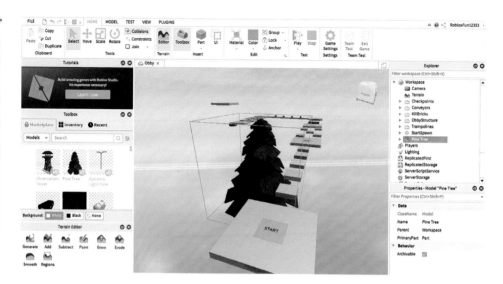

Audio

This allows you to toggle the sounds. This provides you with the ability to turn game sounds on and off in the editor, allowing you to hear what the game will really sound like.

Emulation

Find out how your game performs across different devices. Whether you're using a smartphone of any type, a different computer, a tablet and so on.

Clients & Servers

In order to get a real feel for how the entire game will turn out, it's important to test it in a real server/client environment. That's when you'll see the game the way that other people will view it. Use these tools to do just that!

Simulation

Simulation allows you to perform tasks associated with playing the actual game. This is where you'd start, stop and continue the game play.

MODEL > TOOLS

Snap to Grid

This option is provided at the top tool bar. This function allows you to resize blocks and other objects that you put into the world. To resize the objects, you adjust their numbers and create sizes based off of your world itself.

Parts

Choose the colors, the size, the shape, the look and more with the parts section of the tools that are located at the top of the page. You can group them, anchor them down and more using these tools to help organize your world and all the objects in it.

Solid Modeling

Create complex shapes from simple shapes that you have access to in the builder tool. This is a lot like building complex structures using Legos and it's a lot of fun!

Constraints

This is where you can anchor down the items that you need to keep in the game. Sometimes when things are not anchored down, the players that come into the game are able to change the items and move them.

Gameplay

This allows you to choose special effects that can be used inside the game by the players.

Advanced Feature

This is for those that are more experienced in the game and want tools that allow them to change out items, add new items and even create items from nothing. You can use this if you also know Lua scripting because there is also an option to open up a coding box to put codes into.

TOOLS > PLUGINS

The folder that you open up has a huge number of plugins you can add to the game. You just need to click on the plugin, and it will open up and welcome you to the inside of the game. They will then activate whenever you start up your game.

Animation

The animation portion of this tab allows users to animate rigs or other parts of the game during play. This allows usually non-moving parts to move when they're clicked on.

Generate

You can change the land and how want it to look or how big you want the space to be. This is important because the amount of space and how the land looks is going to change out the way the game looks and feels and if it matches the type of game you are making.

There are specific biomes you can choose from based on the specific game that you are playing.

Add

This tool makes it easy to add specific items to an existing world. Once the box pops up there are many options to choose from that allow you to personalize your world however you'd like.

Subtract

Subtract works almost the same way that an eraser would. It will gradually take away materials starting with a small amount and increasing with each pass you make. To fully remove materials quickly, you'll have to turn the eraser strength up higher before using the tool.

Paint

This seems pretty self-explanatory. If you want to change the look or color of an object that is in the game, you just need to click on this useful little tool, and it is going to do all of the changing that you need it to do. It is just that easy.

Grow

Change out the shape, size and more of the water, land and other features that come with the terrain and look of the background of the game. You can ensure that you get the right look when you can customize the look of the terrain.

Erode

Get to the bottom of things when you are using this feature. This allows you to dig down into the ground. It changes the look and feel of the terrain around you, so you have access to any part of your world and can transform the very landscape that everything is built on.

Smooth

Want a smooth surface to build on? Need to create a road that doesn't have lumps and bumps in it? This is the tool that you would use to smooth out the terrain surfaces, so you don't have to worry about these uneven lands.

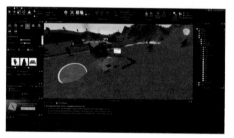

Action

This gives you many different smaller tools in one tool box. You can apply different actions to objects in your game using this tool to create a more dynamic world. You just have to go through the options to choose the one that meets with the needs that you have.

Settings

You can switch out how the game runs and reacts. You want to make sure that the settings are going to go well with your game type. Change the settings and then go to the test section so you can see how the settings have affected your world and what the changes are.

Testing is a must for everyone that wants to make sure their games are running smoothly.

Region

This option allows you to manipulate specific regions of an object. When it comes to adding, removing, changing, or doing anything else within a specific region then this is the best tool to use for that. You want to make sure that you're covering all of your bases and this tool helps you do just that.

Show

Look into the options and changes that you have made in the game using this tool. It helps you take a look at what other people see when they come to visit the game, so it is a must use tool on the list.

Stats

Everyone wants to know how their game is doing and the stats section gives you all the important information. When you go into this section then you are able to learn more about who has come in and who has loved the game or hated the game and more.

HOW-TO START GUIDE

If you decide to create a game of your own, you might not know how to get going. That's why we've assembled this How-To Start guide for you. This guide explains how to get going and how you can begin creating the world you've been dreaming about. Don't worry, it's easier than it seems and before you know it you could be designing and implementing a world of your own that you're proud to show off!

No game is perfect the first couple of times around. The important thing isn't to make something perfect but to get started creating. You'll make something special over time.

With so many different tools and extras that you can make use of, you can effectively change the look and feel of the game that you are making. You'll be amazed at all the different possibilities available to you thanks to all the different tools available in Builder Mode.

ROBLOX

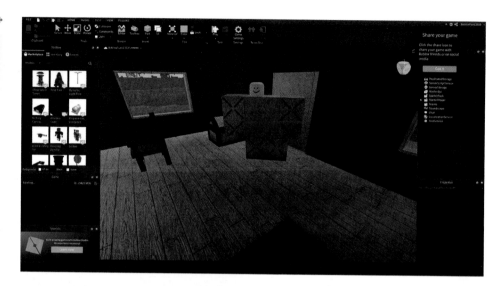

You can choose from all the templates, themes or gameplay. Each of them breaks down the templates into the type of game that you want to create such as combat or obby or if you have a theme such as city or western, then you can find the right theme here for your specific idea.

Whats an obby?

It is one of the most popular games that you will find in Roblox. It is a 3D course that has multiple obstacles that the player has to go through or overcome in order to win at the end. Jumping or moving from one side to the next is often what needs to be done to avoid hazards that are being thrown at you.

An obby is what you would choose if you were to create survival obstacle courses or games like Sonic or Mario.

This is the template we will go with when it comes to making a game, though you can choose any of them. This is just one of the simplest themes to go with when you want to create a game that is not only exciting but fun.

Getting Started

It is easy to get started. You just have to open up the Studio on your computer and you are welcomed with a list of tools in the program and a lot of building space. This is going to be blank for now until you create something to fill in all that available space.

The first step is to choose which template works the best for you. With a handful of options, go with the one that is either the easiest if you do not have a game in mind or the one that is going to fulfill the game needs the best. If you have a good idea for your game, you shouldn't have much trouble choosing the closest template for it.

After you select your desired theme, you're brought into the main game area where you can create things. The best part about this area is that it is super simple to click, drag and drop the items to where you want them. You can also sift through the item catalog on the side to find exactly what you want in the game, but more on that later.

The best part about using a template is that you don't have to worry about creating your own platform. A lot of the pieces are already in place for you to use. You just have to make sure that it is how you want the base game to be. If not, the items can be moved around so that they are in the right place. Simple changes of the obby, and any other theme, are welcomed so that you can make the game your own.

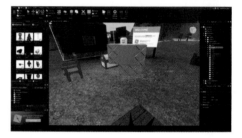

Changing the Time of Day

When you're making the game, you can actually change the time of day using the **lighting feature**. Just click on **Lighting > Properties > Time of Day.** This is located towards the bottom past all of the numbers and data figures. It is going to be in military time, so you have to make sure that you set your time of day using all 24 hours in the day. You can set it for 01:00:00 or you can set it for 18:00:00 or any other time you can think of. The lower numbers below 12 are in the morning, and those past 12 are afternoon hours.

Adding, Removing and More

When you go to create the game, you want to make sure that you're adding, removing and changing things up. The template is just there to be a base. You don't want to make this your whole game, or it might not go so well with the players.

You can change the colors throughout the game with the Color > Edit option at the top of the game. This is a great area to learn more about. You can literally do anything that you want to do in the game using all of the controls at the top of the bar. This is where many players go to change out the items inside the theme that they choose.

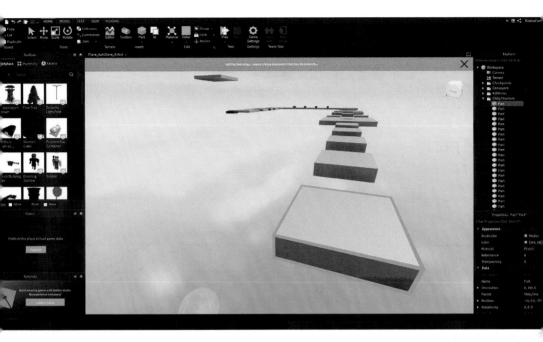

If you want to add new platforms, you just copy them from the menu and paste the new ones to where you want them to be in your game world. It is simple, and this can be done for anything that you find in any of the templates or themes, or for any of the plain games that you start from scratch on. For example: if you want to have a wooded area, but you are in a plain, simple template then you would grab the one or two trees you placed, click copy and then paste it a hundred times until you get the right number of trees that you want in the template.

You can drag anything that you want to move from one place to the next by simply clicking down on the item and then dragging it to where you want it to go. To let go of the item, just unclick and it will drop in the area that you have dragged it over to.

Want to delete something?

When you want to delete something from the game, you can click on the cut option to remove it or you can right click and then click delete. This will remove it from the game, so you don't have to use it or have it there any longer.

The best part about creating a game is being able to customize it exactly the way you want!

There is a whole catalog that you can open up right on the side of the menu in the Builder tool. There are literally thousands of items that you can scroll through and choose to place in your game.

You can use the drop-down menu that is given to section off the items you are looking at to keep everything sorted out. Carefully choose items you want to add into your game using the different theme and category options available. This is something that makes finding the items you want easier. There is also a search bar, so you can type in what you want, and you are then brought to the item easier and quicker.

Once you find the item that you want to put in the game, you just have to click on it. It will then show up on the game and you can click and drag it to the necessary area or place that you want to place it. This provides a nice new item in your game. You can find just about everything and anything that you want to put in any sort of game, regardless of the theme using the powerful catalog.

You can do this as many times as you like until everything is added into your game. Think long and hard about the different objects you want to add to your game to decorate it and you can make it look any way you want!

Finishing Up the Game

If you have created a great game and are happy with everything that you've done, then you need to make sure that you finish it out. This can be done through the Settings tab. Once you finish your game it will be published to the Roblox game area, so you can click through and enter into the game through the website to play.

Settings > File > Publish to Roblox

Name your game, add a description, pictures, videos and anything else that you want that makes it stand out from the rest of the games being offered. You want to make sure to give it a look of its own because you want something that will attract users. Being original gives you the best chance of building up an active following for your game, which helps your game to generate money.

Public or Private

You have the ability to make your game public or private, depending on which fits your needs at the time. This is because some people might not want their game to be public yet, or at all, and being able to have the option to switch between both modes is important.

If you choose to make your game private you'll shut down any currently running games and you'll also cancel any VIP subscriptions that might have signed up for the game.

1. Click on the **Create** button on the top of the website

2. Go to **My Creations** in the tab area and then click on Games

3. Find the world or game that you want to change the settings of and then click on the icon under the title of the place and this is where you can switch between the two settings, either **Private or Public**

Public is the green icon on the bottom of the name, and this allows anyone to come in and play the game that you have made.

Private is the grey icon and it prevents everyone from coming into the game. You are then the only one that has access to the game.

You just need to SAVE the changes that you have just made in order for them to take effect.

LUA QUICK REFERENCE

This Quick Reference guide for Lua will give you some basic commands that you can use to edit your game in small ways. This is not a comprehensive guide, so you might not find all of the codes that are needed to make things happen that you want to really bring your game to life.

There are loads of guides on Lua that you can find and use to your advantage when you want to really make the best game and learn the coding language of Roblox.

One of the best things about Roblox and Lua is that they do provide a tutorial for you to make use of if you want to learn more about Lua at any point.

One of the biggest things to keep in mind is that Lua is a deep language to learn and the Roblox tutorial is not going to teach you everything you need to know. It is simply a quick start guide to give you more information about the program and how you are able to use it when making a game, a good game, that sells.

By letting you know some simple functions, you might be able to get an idea of how the language works and how exactly this is something that can help you make the best game out there.

The more you know Lua, the better your chances are at creating a really good game. There are whole books dedicated to this language and how it works, if you want to create a truly awesome game, we recommend reading more about this programming language.

Roblox's Lua Tutorial

To get to the tutorial, you have to go into the Roblox Studio and right click at the top of the screen, but not on any of the buttons that are up there. This will bring a dropdown menu that provides you with many options. One of the options that should come down is Tutorial. This will then teach you how to do different actions and commands through the game in more depth than what this quick start guide is going to be able to provide.

Screenshot: Roblox® ™ & © 2019 Roblox Corporation

ROBLOX

So where do you type in the scripts that you want to put into the game?

Where exactly does the code go that you will be using?

These are very good questions and probably the most popular question asked by players getting started scripting in Roblox.

The command bar on the side of the screen is where any of the scripts, codes or commands are going to go. There are pre-made ones that you can load into the game, which makes things much easier for everyone, especially those that do not know the language or how to code. However, if you know how to code and understand the syntax and how to put different strings of codes together, you can create more unique games and functions within your game that others might not be able to do. This gives you a serious advantage and makes it possible to create games players will be excited to test out.

The command that you put into the bar should always be lower case. This shows the program that this is the command you want the program to use.

You can put just about anything you can think about inside the command bar, such as ("this is a long test for you to try out")

You can actually give the bar a math question to answer and it will be able to easily answer whatever the equation was that you put into the bar – Lua is just that smart!

>print (2019) is an example that is seen in many of the Lua examples.

You use quotation marks when you have words between the brackets and not numbers. By placing words and sentences inside these brackets, it is known as "strings" in the programming world.

When using code, one of the biggest and best things that you can do is create things that are not shown on the screen in the game but instead change how the game works while remaining invisible. Good quality code is what makes your game function properly, and it's what allows the on-screen objects to behave as they are supposed to.

ROBLOX

When you use the code in the box, you're telling the computer that this bit of information is important to the game and it needs to be able to remember it for when players hop into the game and they want to use the features the code is meant for.

If you want to give it information, you just need to type the information into the box.

For example: TreeNumber = 10

If you want to check to see if the computer remembered this simple bit of information, then you just have to type in a question...

For example: print(TreeNumber) and then the computer should give you the answer 10 because you set the TreeNumber variable to "10". You can use commands like these to keep track of how many objects are in your game world or something else entirely.

This can be done for anything else that is in the game and is being used during that time.

Just remember, the computer is not doing the math on its own, though you could do that if you took some time to teach it simple things such as counting the number of items throughout the game. It only knows what you tell it. You can tell it that the favorite candy for the game is cotton candy or that the number of birds in the trees is six, even if there are no birds.

Lua gives you control over what you tell the game to do and what it should answer. This gives you the power to change your game in any way that you like, but only if you understand how to use Lua properly.

In Roblox Studio, the names of your variables can never start with a number. This is not only the rules of the game, but also the rules of Lua. They cannot have spaces or special characters in the commands or in the names, either. This means pay special attention to how you're typing things into the command bar, because certain phrases and information will not be transferred well.

When you are adding things into the code box, you will notice that the menu might have hidden spots in it that you would find the things you're making within.

For instance, when you go into the 'Workspace' tab on the menu, it is going to open up a bunch of other tabs and when you click those tabs, they open up into other tabs. It is an endless row of tabs that provides multiple functions and options for you to go with.

One of the biggest and best parts about the new Roblox Studio is that when you are typing commands into the box, you do not have to worry about typing the entire word. There will be an autofill option that pops up and you can click on the command you are going for.

Make sure to use periods in between the commands that you put into the bar. A lot of players thought that spaces would work, but this is not the case. You need to make sure that you have the periods in between the commands.

For example: Red = Game.Workspace.ModelColorSpheres.Red

This allows the computer to know that when you are typing red into the game space that you mean the sphere, the red sphere in the game and not anything else. It is a great way to quickly touch on that item or whatever item you put into the game. It does nothing to the outside appearance or functionality of the game but helps with the coding aspects later on behind the scenes when putting the game together.

The autofill function makes it easier to remember different commands and to create code faster and more effectively, and as the tool improves every game creator will benefit. It is helpful for those that do not know the commands on their own and need to use the quick code options that are given in these menus. The tool can help them take their creations a step further without memorizing a bunch of different commands.

TIP: When you are typing in a code like this, you should always remember to type in the name of the object you are referring to first. The name in this instance is red, so you want to start with the name of the object, then the = and then the path that it has to take to reach the object that you are talking about. It is a lot like giving it directions to the destination that you want it to stop at.

Once you understand variables and basic commands, you can do more powerful actions like add multiple numbers together and track important information as the game runs.

For instance: (TreeNumber + 4)

This simple command adds four more trees to your tree count. You can use this information for all sorts of special commands in your Roblox game.

ROBLOX

With that simple command you are telling the computer to do basic math and add more into the game than what was once there before.

You can use scripts for so many different commands and things that can be done inside the game. Lua is very versatile and using it gives you the ability to change anything about your game world that you want.

One of the best things about this programming language is that you not only can change the sizes and colors of the items that are being used in the game, but you can change the material that they are made out of.

Scripts are used in a bunch of different ways throughout Roblox worlds. No matter what you want them to do, you must place them down in the section at the bottom of the game screen. This is where the codes go to change the world.

Scripts are just a fancy name for a set of codes put together to make your game do something. Understanding scripts will let you make important changes to your game world to create the features that your visitors will enjoy in your world.

THESE SCRIPTS OR CHAINS ARE GOING TO LOOK LIKE THIS...

Game.Lighting:SetMinutesAfterMidnight
(7 * 60)

Wait (1)

Game.Lighting:SetMinutesAfterMidnight
(8 * 60)

Wait (1)

Game.Lighting:SetMinutesAfterMidnight
(9 * 60)

Wait (1)

Game.Lighting:SetMinutesAfterMidnight
(10 * 60)

Wait (1)

Game.Lighting:SetMinutesAfterMidnight
(11 * 60)

Wait (1)

Game.Lighting:SetMinutesAfterMidnight
(12 * 60)

ROBLOX

This simple script changes the lighting throughout the game while someone is playing. By adding this command to your game you've taught the game to control the lighting all on its own, which is more than others can say for the changes they can make in their game. As long as you use the correct commands and you type them out with periods instead of spaces in between the words, you can make the game react just the way you want it to.

You can do this type of script or chain with any other function that you want to have happen throughout the game. Keep this in mind when going through and changing up all of these areas. You can make your own commands happen with the use of the right codes placed in the command bar on the screen in Roblox Studio.

You're the one in control and you're the one making the game happen.

There are two places that you can do this coding in the Roblox Studio. You've been using the Command Bar throughout this entire tutorial, but you can also use the Output area that is a part of the creator, as well. This second option is where you can see the effects take

hold right away. For beginners, the first option is usually the best until you become familiar with the creator and with the language that is being used to create.

If you're looking for a great way to build and make the most of the fun that you are going to have, start with the Roblox Lua guide to learn a lot of great coding tips and tricks. Familiarizing yourself with this awesome language will help you gain even more knowledge in the game making world than ever before.

Even though this wasn't an in-depth look into all that you can do with this language, it still provides you with the base that is needed to help you decide whether you want to learn Lua or not. When this is something that you want to do, make sure to make Lua a priority when the time comes. You want the best world possible and knowing how to program with Lua is the only way to achieve your goals.

ROBLOX

If you're into coding and want to know more about making your own video games, then Lua is the language to start with and learn. Roblox is there to help you with all of the coding you want to do along the way.

There are many things to think about when it comes to creating a game. When you want to make the most out of the game, the money you are trying to make, and the fun you're giving those that come to stop in and have a good time then these quick start things are something you need to learn more about.

When you are having a good time in Roblox, remember that someone made that game you are enjoying. Creating an entertaining game is something you can do as well. It's something that anyone can do, when they take a little time to get to know more about the creator and the language that the games are made in. Simple to use and even simpler to throw a game together. The Roblox builder is an easy tool and can help you create a game that others will pay to play.

Hopefully the above guide gives you something to think about if you decide you want to create your own games for Roblox. It's easy to get started creating Roblox games, but it takes time to master all the different tools and the scripting language you need to make more advanced creations. Take some time to learn Lua and what you can do with it, learn to use the Builders tools and you'll be well on your way to creating fantastic games that players will want to try for themselves.

Everyone is welcome to try their luck at creating their own games, and if you get good enough you could even make a name for yourself in the Roblox community!

RoBLoX

Iamwillyk

hoots88889999

Claim L

[1] Manage

2] Supply

3] Upgrade

4] Workers

5] Furnish

6] Build

Scripting with Lua in Roblox for More Fun!

We merely glanced over Lua scripting in our previous chapters while explaining how valuable it can be for creating impressive games. That's why we decided to assemble this chapter for you, taking a closer look at Lua scripting and how to use it to your full benefit when creating a new game. This is a step-by-step guide on doing some simple scripting of your own and should help you become more comfortable with the idea of Lua and how it can help with your game projects. This will just dive a bit deeper into the scripting. Spend a minute reading through this chapter and you'll be excited at the possibilities.

Of course, if you don't get scripting right away, that's okay too!

Not everyone catches on the first time while trying to create their own scripts. It definitely takes practice and time, as well as lots of reading and trial and error to get better. You know what they say though, nothing worth doing comes easy!

If you want to learn Lua, just stick with it. If you can do that, you'll soon be able to code anything you want in Roblox and bring your world to life in the process.

SCRIPTING

Scripting is simply writing a series of Lua commands to tell the program what to do. The things you can make the game do are limitless, which is why understanding how to create scripts makes you a better Roblox game developer instantly.

Lua is less powerful than other scripting languages out there such as Ruby or Python, but it's also simpler to learn and is powerful enough to help you create the important changes you want most for your programs. A scripting language like Ruby especially requires more instruction and understanding to learn to use, and can be pretty difficult to master.

SETTING UP TO SCRIPT

Go to Roblox Studio and make sure that all of the below options are set on open. They usually are by default, but it is important to double check in order to successfully be able to script.

> View>Output
> View>Explorer
> View>Properties
> View>Toolbars>Command

Scripting works best when you aren't actually playing your game. So, you want to choose the RUN option instead of the PLAY option. You just need to click on the down arrow that you can find right under the PLAY button. It should then be set to the green arrow, not the blue arrow.

CREATING A SCRIPT

To create a script, you need to first make a new place, or edit an existing place using the Studio option. Once you are in a new place, give it a unique name so you know how to refer to it.

Go to the EXPLORER box and then **Workspace>Insert Object** and select the **Script** option. Do not choose the Local Script option, that is also next to the name. You should then see the script in the workspace that you have.

Double click on the box to view the script that is in it. It should look like this:

print 'Hello World!'

To test your new script, simply click on the Play button. Hello World! Should appear on the Console/ Output log area of the screen.

Print is the function used in the box. Hello World is the parameter or the value that you can manipulate to change your game.

Variables in scripting can change, they are not constant values. One example of variables is this:

```
a = 5                    5
b = "Hello World!"    >> Hello World!
c = a                    5
print(a)
print(b)
print(c)
```

In this example a, b and c are all the variables. You are assigning them the values "5". "Hello World!" and "a". These values can be changed to be something else later. Right now, a is equal to 5, b is equal to the characters "Hello World!" and c is also equal to "5". Change the values of any of the variables and they will be equal to something else instead.

Notice how "Hello World!" is put into quotations while the number values are not. That's because strings, or a list of characters must be kept in quotes.

Wondering why both a and c were equal to 5 in the above example? That's because a is equal to 5 and c was set to be equal to a, so they are the same value.

Usually a script command is set up like this
FUNCTION_NAME(PARAMETERS_TO_FOLLOW)

PRACTICE BY REMOVING A CHARACTERS HEAD

There are many ways to practice Lua scripts, but one of the more entertaining options is to remove a character's head. This is just a simple task that we are going to do to give you some practice using this language.

Type this into the script box:

game.Workspace.Player.Head:remove( ) —DAI

Do not click the RUN or PLAY button this time. Instead, you want to click on Home > Test > Play. This should be shown as a blue arrow on the screen and a Roblox sign in the middle of it.

Spawn into the game as you usually would, but you're going to be shown inside the game as "Player." The chat bar is going to disappear, and you will still be able to use the Studio while you are scripting this, even without a head.

As soon as you spawn into the game, you should spawn in without a head.

How did this happen?

Simply put...

Game is at the top of the command, and it has to be done in order because this is how Roblox functions. It reads the entire script from beginning to end in order to change your game. When you put in game, it is essentially saying that this should be done inside this game.

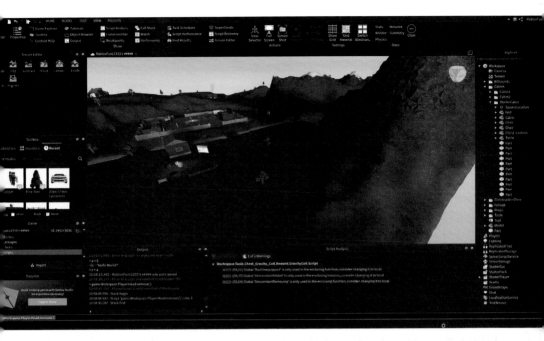

The period in between the commands shows that you are moving on to the next command that you want to execute.

The Workspace is the next command after game, and this shows that this should be done in the Workspace of the game. Player is the character that you want to have the head removed from. This would normally be someone's name, but since you are just Player in this game, it is set as that.

Head is your head and remove is the command you are enacting on the head object. You want it to be removed.

It is also important to note that in Lua there are comments that you can use to explain your script. These special lines of code are ignored entirely by the computer, and only meant for the programmers reading the script. Comments also give you a way to quickly cancel out blocks of code during testing. Comment out a line to see how the world changes without that code.

If you want to comment many different lines of code out, then you will want to start with:

`--[[`

If you want to continue the multi-line comment, then you will have to make sure to add at the end of it:

`]]--`

If you wanted to create a script using these in the comments section, then it would look something like this:

`--]]`

This code will not run and is just for show.

`]] –`

FINDING A PRODUCT IN THE GAME

If the script is saying that something is unable to be found, you have an error that you need to correct before it will work properly. In this instance, an 'if' block is the solution to make the code work properly.

```
character = game.
Workspace:findSmallChild("bigbabyone")
--Find him..

if character ~= nil then --Does he exist?

character.Head:remove() --If so, remove him.
>:D

end
```

There are a lot of terms in the above script that explain to the computer exactly what it should be doing, and how it should be doing it.

It is essentially a series of commands that are used in the game to make precision changes one after another. The script is telling the game to find a specific player inside the game, and if they do exist in the game, the computer must remove him from the game.

If the player is not there, that is the end of the script and it will not do anything else. The command will stop there.

A single = sign means that you are setting the value of a certain variable or choosing what the variable means, while a double == indicates that you are checking for a certain value. .

Instead of end, the end of the script would be the]] -- and the beginning would be the --]] as mentioned earlier in this section about scripting.

CHANGING OBJECT PROPERTIES

If you want to change the properties of the objects in your game, then you need to make sure that your script has the proper commands in it. You might not want to just cut off heads or print endless supplies of pizza. Whatever it is, there is a way to script changes into your world, so it behaves exactly the way you want it to. You can even do something like take control of another user in the game or change the time of day in your world at will.

To have your world change its time of day, you have to consider the location of the lighting and whether you will be able to influence the lighting using your script. Lighting is the parent of the script in this case, and not the child. This is because lighting is above what you want the other option to be, making it the parent and 'in control' of the other option. The idea of parent objects and child objects is a confusing one to master, but just keep in mind that parent objects can influence child objects, while child objects have no power over parent objects. Remember that and you'll find it easier to create working scripts.

script.Parent

Whenever you input a script command, make sure your first word is all lowercase, but that the command after the period starts with a capital letter. Lua is funny like this and your scripts won't run properly if you don't follow this important naming rule.

You can do a little research to find out what you want to do with the lighting and what the script command would be for it. In this case, I have already done the research and to change the time of day, we would have to add "TimeOfDay" into the command field.

script.Parent.TimeOfDay

You then have to change it to the time of day that you want it to be on. This is shown using a simple number value. If you want it to be night time, then this would be a 0 and increasing the number moves your game through all the hours of the day one after another with an increased value.

script.Parent.TimeOfDay = (0)

You can also change the time of day to lighting by replacing the Parent to Lighting. This will then change out the lighting function and the area that the script is able to change.

ADDING NOTES TO YOUR SCRIPT

You can also add notes to your script so that you can go back and remember what you were doing or trying to do. Simply add in some lines of comments in order to do this. The comments do not make the game do anything at all, and only serve as a reference for readers that look at your script.

script.Parent = "NOTWORKING"

AGH NOTWORKING SCRIPT.Workspace. R700:Destroy( ) bigfluff

Game.Lighting.TimeOfDay = (10000000000 0000000000000.00000001)

WOOT Goodjob

nothing else

    end

end

end

print "Cows Can Fly"

To add this script to your game and adjust the time of day of your game add the newest command to your script box and see how it transforms your world.

Screenshots: Roblox® ™ & © 2019 Roblox Corporation

Comments are helpful commands and you should use them whenever you want to remember why you put in part of your script. Add in comments whenever you create new code for your script, and you won't have to guess at what you were thinking at the time.

```
script.Parent = "NOTWORKING"

AGH NOTWORKING SCRIPT.Workspace.
R700:Destroy() bigfluff

Game.Lighting.TimeOfDay = (10000000000
0000000000000.00000001)

WOOT Goodjob -- This makes it not work
(by turning this line into a comment), so
remember to fix it (by removing the dashes)

nothing else

     end

end

end

print "Cows Can Fly"
```

There are many different scripts and codes that you can implement in your worlds. Whenever you come up with an advanced idea for one of your game worlds, remember the changes you want to make to your world, and use scripts to help you make those changes. Advanced worlds almost always require scripts to work properly, which is why so many game makers spend hours learning how to script for their worlds.

Coding is fun to do, and it's a tool you should try and make the most of for the sake of your world. With Roblox, you can create the best look and provide new exciting functions for players that come and use your game.

Be unique and create a game that is different from the others out there. Use advanced scripts to show off your unique personality and creativity and to help you create something other players will be excited to try out.

Scripting can take some time to get used to, but once you do, you're set to take on just about any game or program that you want to create because you have the knowledge and the power to make your world behave however you want! Learning to script will also make it easier to learn new languages later on down the road if you choose to code with those, as well.

Happy coding!

Making Money with Your Own World

Everyone loves playing Roblox games, and you might even enjoy creating them, but did you know you can actually make money from them?

If your games are good enough, you can make some cash and invite people to come in and be a part of your world. New players can come in and become members of the game you invented and created on your own. There's nothing better than that!

Many kids come to Roblox to play exciting games created by others. Some will come to your world to play after creating something themselves. Often, they create games without ever publishing them. Is that the kind of player you want to become? Of course not! That's why it's so important to learn how to create effective games, and how to make money with those games. We covered creating top-quality games in an earlier chapter, and we're going to go over how to make money in your own world.

First you have to know how to create your own world. Once you understand that, you need to know how to make the most of your creation. After you've finished your brilliant new creation, you can ask visitors to pay to come in or you can sell in-game items and perks to them.

We've also added some awesome tips and tricks for creating your world, so you know exactly how to create something you're proud of, and how to make the most of your creation as well.

Are you ready to create your own world?

CREATING YOUR OWN WORLD

Before you can make money off your world, you have to create it. This is the most difficult part of the process and the step that you really need to perfect. Follow our simple guide to create something special that other players are sure to enjoy. Once you do that, you'll have a better chance at making money from your game whether you charge people for entry or you sell off items from within your game once they arrive.

ROBLOX

There are some steps that you must take before you can make the ultimate game and reap the benefits of creating a world that's special and unique.

Formulate an Idea

Every good game starts with a unique idea that you build on. Before you can create your game, you need to come up with an awesome idea to base it on. If you already have an amazing idea you can skip ahead to building the game. If not you should visit popular games, talk with other players on Roblox and try to find out what they are interested in. With enough research you should be able to create an awesome idea to base your game on. Don't rush this process though. The idea is everything, and a good idea will sell your game more than anything else that you do.

Create the Game!

You've thought of a great idea and you want to make sure that it works, so you have to create it to perfection. This process is time-consuming, but it's also the fun part. You get to see your ideas come to life!

Start off by opening up the Roblox Creator and selecting a template based off of the game that you want to make. If you can't find a template you want to use you can also create the game from scratch. You'll have to adjust all the elements of the game yourself and it will take more time without a starting template, but you'll also end up with a more unique creation in the end for your added efforts.

Create > Template or No Template

Start by adding, removing, or changing the things in the world you decide need to be changed from the original template. You'll have to follow different steps depending on the template you decide to go with here.

All the tools you need are located at the top of the screen. You can sort through the options, changes and other available features by using the menu up at the top of the builder screen. It's a powerful resource, so take some time to get comfortable using it!

You can insert items into the game with the upper left section of the builder menu at the top. All the tools in the builder make it possible to create any game you like, just take the time to explore the different options and get comfortable with what each of them does for your world.

Play around with different looks and items throughout the game as well to help you get ideas that you can use for your game. Much of creating a unique world is testing out building materials you insert and swapping them out until you find a look you like.

Continue that cycle of trying out different items, swapping in new options and slowly deciding on the permanent elements of your world that will help it to stand out.

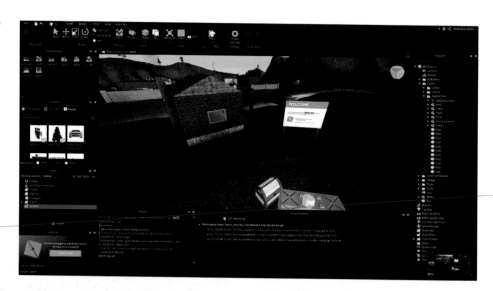

Adding Extras

You will have a section that allows you to add in shirts, hats, gear, pants, decals, models, game passes, badges, body parts and packages for you to switch through. Think about the extras that will go with the theme of your game and get other players excited about what you have to offer. Now test out different elements from this menu and have friends come in and try them out as well. Take time to decide which of these special extras are right for your world.

Adding badges is one of the best ways that you can enhance your game. With badges you give your player base goals to try and achieve. The badges work like achievements, and they add a purpose to your world. A good badge system keeps players coming back to your world again and again, because it gives them trophies to work towards. Even just a few well thought-out badges can help make your creation into a success.

Creating games isn't difficult if you understand how to use the builder and you have a plan.

While we are not going to walk through the game creation step by step here, as a lot of the other sections explain what to do in more depth, you want to create a game that will sell well to other players. To do this you can use of the templates, the add-ons, the extras and more. Knowing more about scripting will help your chances as well and work to improve the quality of your final creation.

It is important that you create a game you want to play. It will take you some time to go through the many different tools offered by the Builder, but after taking the time to learn, you can customize and personalize nearly everything in the world.

ROBLOX

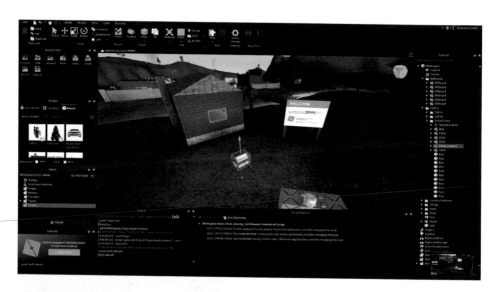

Utilize scripts to enhance your games and add the features you're most interested in. With scripts you can make your game react in any way you like. When someone plays the game, you need to make sure that it is going to be able to interact and change where it needs to. Scripts make this possible, and the right scripts will help your game behave just the way you want it to.

Scripts are available through the menu actions at the top, or you can learn to type in commands all on your own using the Roblox tutorial. Take time to learn how Lua works and how to make use of scripts and you'll enhance your games dramatically.

To learn more about this useful scripting language you can get educational help from Roblox themselves through the Roblox Education program. Roblox Education is offered in their schooling section and they welcome one and all that want to learn how to code with Lua to come in and have a good time learning more about what the language has to offer and how it can improve your games. Learn to harness the powerful language and transform your games for the better.

Once you go through the game and you have it set up how you want, or how you think you want, you must go through the next steps to make sure it works properly and that it's high-quality. This is important because a game that performs smoothly and without any bugs will be enjoyed by more players and gain followers faster helping it be successful.

Good luck!

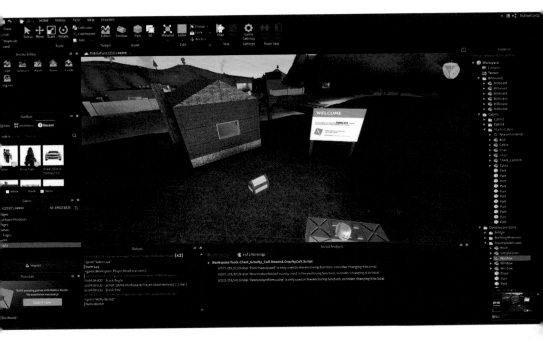

Test, Test and then Test Again!

One of the final steps of creating a high-quality game is testing it to be sure it works properly. Start by testing the game yourself. Once you test it, then you want to make sure that you test it again. Testing and re-testing your game gives you a chance to catch any issues with it that might slip past you and ruin the play experience for other players.

Have someone else test it after you test it a few times. Have some friends go in and check it out. They can give you some insight on what you should add, remove or even change in the game to make it more entertaining or let you know if things are not working how they should. Having a test group is important for creating a game that's going to perform well.

Share Your Game

Once you've done all of the above steps you need to share your game with the world. Share your new game far and wide and you're sure to get at least a few players in to try it out. If it's a good enough creation your player base will expand over time as well and put you in a position to make money off your creation.

Sharing your games is one of the biggest ways to invite people to come and play the game and to hopefully have a good time with your creation. However, it shouldn't be shared until you are absolutely ready to share it. It should be heavily tested and running smoothly before you have gamers come in and test things out. That's the only way you'll build a following for your creation!

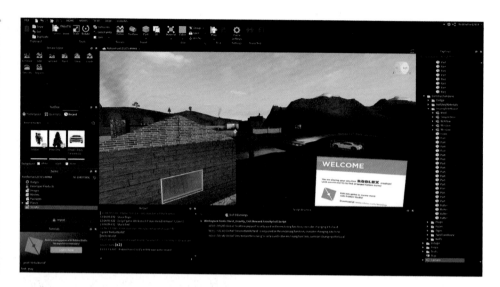

Take Your Time

Make sure to take your time when creating your world or game. Taking some extra time will help ensure that the game will run as smoothly as possible. When it does, you will feel great about being able to share something you're proud of with others around you.

Making a game that everyone can remember and that brings them back time and time again is so important. You want something that will make you money, but if the game is not good, no one is going to want to come try it out. Not only will they avoid your game even when it's free, but they definitely won't pay to play your creation.

Keep this in mind while you go through the steps to create your new game. The only way it's going to hit the front page of Roblox and make everyone want to come in and have a good time is if you take your time and create something special. It can be done, but you have to really work to create something impressive and that other people can connect with.

It's not as hard as you think to do, but it does take time and hard work.

ASK VISITORS FOR AN ENTRANCE FEE

Asking for Robux is something many players do once they complete making their worlds or game and they have a success. It's important to get more from your game when it's complete, but you also need to make sure that the game is worth what you charge. This is one of the biggest things to think about when it comes to creating a game, deciding what to charge for it and making money from your creation.

There is a quick way to ask visitors that come into your game to pay an entrance fee. This is done in the Creator area while you are making the game.

There is a section at the top that provides options and opens a dropdown menu. Use this to set an amount for the access section in the game. You want to make sure that this is done before making the game live, otherwise players can get in and play for free if the setting isn't checked. Remember, if you are trying to test the game out, use the "friends only" mode so that others are unable to get into the game when you are working on it.

If Roblox notices you are offering a game for any amount of money and that game has nothing in it or it does not provide any real value, then it is going to be booted off the board so that no one can enter it except for you. They do not want to have their players coming into a game and paying for it if it is not worth the money you're asking for. This is a waste of money and will lead to a poor experience for Roblox players, which is something the creators certainly want to avoid. They work hard to protect players from this sort of outcome from ever occurring.

You can choose between 25 and 100 Robux for an entrance fee, but it is important that you think about how much you would pay to go into and play the game you made. The money that the players pay should be worth what you are asking them to pay. You don't want to overcharge someone for a game that is not worth it.

Remember, if there are an excessive amount of complaints made on your game then the developers will go into the game and check it out. If the complaints are true, then they will quarantine your game and you'll have the chance to change everything about the game that needs to be changed. If these issues are not addressed, then the game can be completely removed, and players won't have access to it any longer.

One Time Purchases

There are vending machines that you can have placed in the game. This will help you provide a way for you to offer purchases to your visitors in a simple way. Everyone is free to come to the machine, choose what they want to purchase and then purchase it. Keep in mind, you will need to know some scripts in order to set up one of these machines with the items you're interested in selling.

There are scripts for shirts, hats, game passes and more. If you can think it, you can find a script for it and you can sell it.

Once added to the machine, the person that comes into the game will be prompted to pay for the purchase that they make through the machine. To complete the purchase, they can use their account balance, or if they don't have enough funds they will be prompted to add more to their account.

CREATE A GAME PASS

A Game Pass is a powerful tool that either allows players to get into your world or makes them special VIP members of your world.

Go to the Roblox Website > Create > My Creations > Games

Use the dropdown menu on the right-hand side of the page to go to Create Game Pass option.

In order to create a game pass, you must open up the pass creation section and choose pass options that fit your game best. Then, you just have to use your creativity to make something that stands out for the game. This is the pass that shows they paid for their entrance or VIP section in your game. The passes are circles and you can create any look that you want.

You have to set the price that you want the pass to be for, so everyone knows what they're paying for access to the game. The price you choose to put on the pass is going to affect the people that come and purchase it. Going with a lower number will make your pass accessible to more people and will result in more people buying it, but it's up to you to decide on an amount that balances affordability with being profitable for you. Choose the right amount to charge and you'll help tons of players access your special features while bringing in a pile of Robux for you.

Make sure that you save the options you put on the pass. This will ensure that you are able to keep the settings and changes that you made for your game pass.

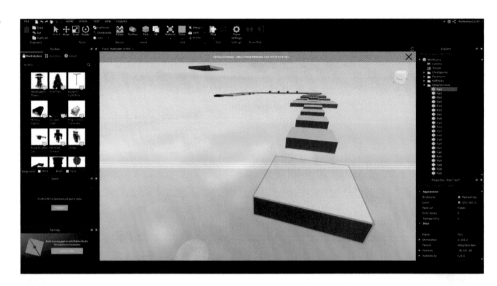

You can also configure the settings of this specific game, create badges in this area, add gear to sell or give for free, advertise or sponsor the game that you are putting up for the general public.

TIPS & TRICKS FOR OPENING YOUR OWN GAME TO THE PUBLIC

There are many different tips and tricks for creating your own game and then opening it up to the public. If you want to make cash with it, this can be done, as well.

All of these tips can help you get the most from the game that you choose to play and offer more to the players that come in for a good time. By keeping all those potential visitors in mind while creating your game, you'll have a better chance of creating something truly outstanding.

Make sure to plan out the game and world that you want to create, so you'll have a clear idea of what to create during the rest of the building process.

Write down a series of ideas before you go with one. The best games are built on clever ideas, and by writing down your ideas you'll come up with more. You want to expand on those ideas and then go with the one that you can expand the most and the one that seems the most interesting and exciting to create from.

If you create a game you wouldn't pay to play yourself, then it is probably a game that won't do well with visitors either.

Make a game that makes the players work for it. You want to give them goals and objectives that they need to complete in order to win the game. The more you give them, the more likely they are to have a good time playing your game.

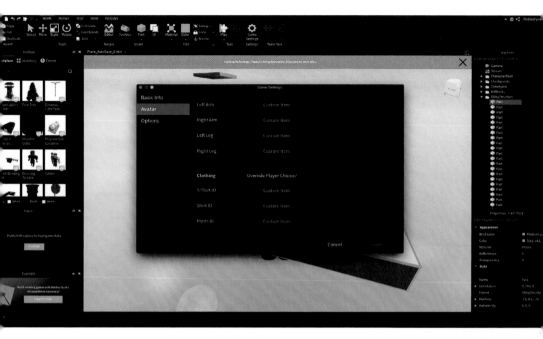

Create a weekly checklist, or a checklist in general of what needs to be done for your game, so you don't fall behind and so that everything gets done on the list that needs to get done. You want to make sure that this is something you work towards almost every day to help finish your game efficiently.

Do not use too many free items in your game because that can lead to excessive lag. Free items are often poorly optimized and with many in place you might experience slowdowns and choppiness as you play. No one wants to play a lagging game and chances are, players will leave once the game starts to lag.

Learn how to create your own models through scripting if you want to offer something unique that other creators don't have. This is how new things start in the games and how games get features that aren't currently available. The more familiar you are with Lua, the better your game is going to be.

Putting items on sale during an event can entice players to come in and purchase items in your game world. Usually when something is on sale, they are more likely to purchase the items and there will be many more people coming and going from the game, due to the event and the sale.

Even if you're selling things in the game, you still need to make the game fun to play. No one is going to come into a game and buy anything if the game isn't fun. You can even sell items in your game that don't have much of a purpose at all, as long as your game is enjoyable, and players want to keep coming back. Add stylish outfits and accessories to your game and happy players will purchase them.

Keep the gameplay in mind first and foremost because you want to make sure that you are creating a game that is actually fun to play. It's up to you to focus on making your game enjoyable. If you spend too much time thinking about how to make money from your game, but not enough making it entertaining, it's doomed to fail eventually.

Always have items that are known as cosmetic items. These are character items that you should have for sale in the game. Cosmetics are a favorite for most players and having them makes sure that everyone that is playing the game, whether free or not, is not left behind. Everyone has the opportunity to cash in on the awesome products that you have to offer them. Plus, this is one of the easiest and best ways to make money with your game.

Make sure to pay attention to what is working in your game and what is not. Take note of all these things so you can make improvements to your creation until it's something most people will enjoy playing. Even if the first or even second game that you make doesn't do as well as you would like, you can still benefit from them by learning about your mistakes and how you can prevent them from happening in the future.

Your game can be removed if you do not provide a fun experience or the experience that you have listed in the description of the game. This is important to think about. If you are offering a specific game and you are letting the players that come in know more about it, but fail to deliver on what you say, then the players can complain. If enough complain and nothing is fixed on your end, your game will be removed, and the players will then be refunded their money from your account.

Don't make this a job and have fun with it! You want to make sure that you're enjoying creating games and flexing that creative muscle. If you're only doing this for the money or the Robux, then forget about creating something that sells. You need to have fun and enjoy the game to make something everyone else is going to love playing.

Make sure to advertise your games and let others know about them! This is one of the biggest and best ways to get the word out and let others know that they even exist. The forum and chats are a great way to spread the word and get more from what is being offered in your game!

If you are going to be making a game, keeping these tips in mind will help your creation. You want to make a game that everyone is going to enjoy, but you need to make sure that you prepare yourself for the creation process and all it requires from you. This is something that needs to be done with some pretty good planning.

Once you take the time to look through the tips and tricks and go through a tutorial or read some of our quick start guides that are found in this book, you should have no issues creating a game. Whether or not it is good depends on your imagination and what ideas you come up with and how much time you spend creating your game.

ROBLOX

Game Developers are Making Thousands of Dollars

The top producing game developers for Roblox are making thousands upon thousands of dollars by creating games that sell.

With a monthly cap of $2,000 per game for players creating their own games, there is a good amount of money to be made with Roblox game development. Additionally, if developers have made $10,000, they can cash all of that money out. While this seems like a big jump, it is one that will help the really good game makers make even more with their creations.

You can make a living with Roblox if you are able to gain up to $10,000 per month by selling access, VIP passes and other items within the game. When you do this, you're giving those players something fun to do but you're also creating a living for yourself, regardless of how old you are or how much Lua you know!

Roblox was once just a fun game that can be played but now with so many developers that are throughout the game, you can find a way to learn more about creating games from the backend of the game and create something special that stands out.

There are even Roblox developers that are kids just like you, making $100,000 per year with the games that they are putting out there for other players. With such a high earning potential that literally any of the players are able to reach, it makes you wonder why so many other players haven't tapped into this potential.

Many of the lower money-making developers are still making around $300 per month off of the game, which is still great money for a game that you put together and have fun on. Everyone is able to do this and have a good time doing so with enough hard work, research and advancements.

Roblox is working hard to make its platform more enjoyable for everyone. By adding other ways to play the game, they are expecting to bring in more of an audience. Their expansion to other countries should help to increase the Roblox audience as well. Roblox is going to be bigger and better than ever and able to provide the players with a larger base to offer their game and purchases to.

When the time comes to make the most of the game that you make, just make sure that you know what you are doing, how you are doing it and that you are trying to make the best game out there.

Who knows, you might just make a game that is bigger and better than MeepCity!

If you do make one bigger than that, we are proud of you and knew you could do it all along!

While we are working on our game, you can be sure to work on yours and everything that comes along with it. Be a part of something awesome when the time comes. Make a game that is fun to play and then share it with us because we would love to see what you have thought of!

Happy creating and happy playing!

ROBLOX

Press 1 2

Crow
6

Tips for Creating Games That Sell

Developer

Monthly Event Game Application

This survey is not accepting additional responses at this time. Thank You!

Now that you have learned how to use creative mode and learned how and why you should create games that sell, you should have an idea of how to create games that sell effectively.

You want to create games that others are going to want to play and visit. They are not going to give you Robux to come into your world if it isn't any fun!

Fun should be your main goal. Make something that everyone is going to want to come in and check out. Really stick with an idea and make it happen, no matter how hard it might seem to get to work.

So how exactly do you get people to play the games that you make?

How do you make money off of these games that you create and put together?

The top grossing game makers let us know what they do to bring people in and make some Robux off of the games they make. Whether you want to cash in with the money you make from the games, or if you want to use it in the game, there are many options for you to make the most of the Robux that you make while making a game that is offered to all of the players of the game.

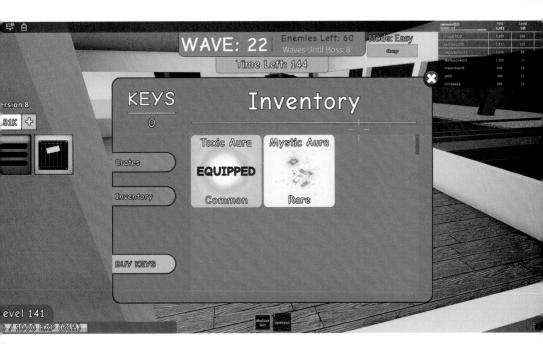

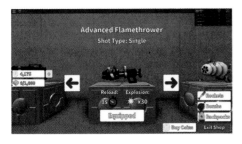

MAKING YOUR GAMES POPULAR ON ROBLOX

There are a few different things you should go through to make your games popular on Roblox. This is important because if you make a game and you put a price on it, you're still not going to be able to make money if you are unable to get anyone in to play the game.

Making an Icon

The first step to making a popular game is creating a nice icon for it. The icon is the welcoming picture that people will see when they search through the games. It is a badge that stands out and makes the game stand out. Make sure to choose a clear, colorful picture that is well framed and gives your game an image.

If you need further help creating an icon, the developer section on the Roblox website offers a helpful guide to walk you through the process. You can learn more about thumbnails, icons and even uploading videos that showcase your game to everyone.

Add Images or Videos to Your Game

If you're looking into showing off your game to those that come to look at it, you need to add a video or pictures to the front screen. This shows everyone what the game is about, and you can even make a nice video that shows off the features of the game and acts as a preview that helps to draw in new players.

The developer section on Roblox where the icon tutorial is located also has information about adding photos and videos to the front page of your Roblox game. Read through this helpful section to learn how to make your game stand out.

The Game Matters

In order to bring people to your game you need to make sure that the game you make is one people want to play. If people come to your game, regardless of how nice the video, pictures or icons are, they are not going to come back or tell other people about the game if they don't have a good time playing it. You want to make sure that you create an entertaining experience for your visitors. For some that means creating an opportunity to socialize with other players, and for others that means offering excellent gameplay that captures the attention and provides goals to achieve.

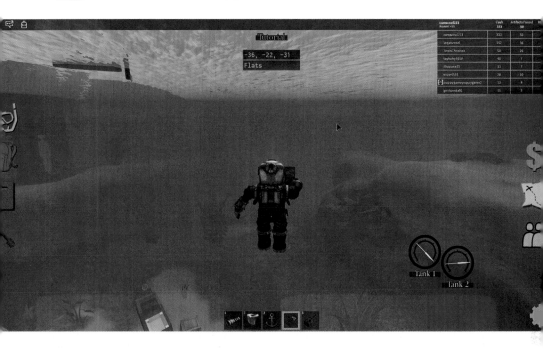

Make a game you'd want to play with your friends and one you could find yourself coming back to playing time and time again. Do that and you're on the right path to creating a game that actually sells.

If you want to check out all that comes with other games before you make yours, the developers strongly recommend that you look and see what other people are doing and even asking some people in the games what types of games they would like to see. This opens up more options for you to choose from and make.

Game Passes and VIP Shirts

Give out something special to players that spend Robux to get these special items in your game. You want to make sure that you're offering something special when bringing people in because everyone wants to have a chance to have something to show off. You can hand out shirts that not everyone has if they sign up to become a VIP. The game passes can offer special powers that not everyone in the game has as well as giving them a very good incentive to spend a bit on your game.

Talk with Many, Many Players

If you are not regularly social with the players of the game, then you might not know what they like. Like mentioned above, it is very, very important that you get out of your comfort zone to find out what the other players are into and looking to play. You want to find out what games other players prefer to play and more.

ROBLOX

One of the best places that you can go to do this is on the forum. This is a place where you can provide everyone with updates on the game that you are making.

Instead of saying come and play my game, let everyone know what changes you made since you last were on and also make sure that they know what you're trying to accomplish. By creating an audience, or a following, you're allowing yourself to reach many more people.

You can also show off your game on YouTube, on the game itself, through Facebook and other areas. Make sure to ask players to come in and test the game for you and then provide feedback once you do. This will help you change the things that might need to change. You might not be able to see what needs to be changed without having an outside source telling you what they think should be changed. Perhaps give an elite few a pass to the game to play and provide the feedback.

Advertise as Much as You Can!

There are many ways that you can grab the attention of those that might want to play the game. Advertising is one of the best ways to go about this.

If you're unsure of what advertising is, then read through our descriptions to learn about the different types and how they are used. Roblox is there providing all that you need to work on this and do this for yourself, as well as having a support system that provides the help that is needed when you are trying to tell everyone about the game that you have created that is now available.

There are many parts in the developer section of the Roblox website that gives detailed information on how to do all of the advertising that you want to do, but we are going to go over a few of the options that you have for advertising to get a better idea of each.

Word of Mouth: Word of mouth is one of the best ways to get the word out about your game. Putting it on the forums is one of the best ways to spread the word. You want to let everyone know about the game you made, so throw it out there in the forums, in group chats, in other games and more.

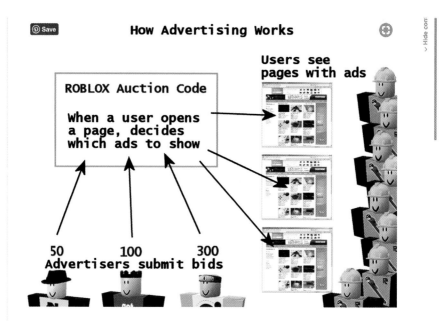

How Advertising Works

ROBLOX Auction Code

When a user opens a page, decides which ads to show

Users see pages with ads

50   100   300
Advertisers submit bids

Advertisers don't buy ad space on Roblox. They bid for it in an auction. There is a limited amount of ad space to go around (we only show so many ads per day), so

Sponsored Games: These sponsored games get ad space that is shown in other games. It shows that it is sponsored but looks just like the other ads and games that are out there. This option though costs Robux in order to get in the bidding system for your game to be shown on the ads.

The person that bids the most money is the one that is going to get the most slots and time in those slots. If you think you have something awesome to show off, then this is definitely the way you want to go.

Once you create a game there is an option to have it sponsored with the website, so you can have it shown off. Once it is sponsored, you can check the results of the promotion from your Sponsored Games tab.

User Ads: These are ads that come up on the website itself that show off the clothing, animations or the games that you have created. You're able to create the ad image of your choice because they give the developers or game makers free range of how their ad looks before they run it.

BLOX

Roblox Support > Building on Roblox > Advertise Your Game

Search

Articles in this section

How to Make Ads

Sponsored Games

Game Thumbnails, Videos, and Icons

Video Advertisement Policy

Developer Statistics

Buying and Selling Places

How To Make Your

How to Make Ads

Once you have created the game, group or piece of clothing of your dreams, it's time to get the word out so that other players can start enjoying the fruit of your labors. While word of mouth is a powerful tool on its own, Roblox offers several tools to help get you started. One of these tools is the User Ads feature.

What are user ads?

Ads are images that players upload that can be use to promote their places, clothing, models, decals, groups, etc. These will be displayed at the top and sides of Roblox.com. When the image is clicked, it will take you to the thing that is being advertised.

Advertising is a good way to bring attention to the awesome stuff that you have built or made. You may even be able to make Robux by bidding on ads for an item which other players may then purchase or visit.

Just like the sponsored games section for advertising, this section also uses the same bidding and auction system. Robux are added to the account and you can bid either a lot or a little to try to outbid the other developers that are looking to win the same space.

Advertise your games in so many different ways. You want to make sure that you choose the best method to get the game you made out and with so many options available through Roblox, you can choose one or all to go with when you are trying to get more players to come in.

Don't start using these advertisement methods until you have the game created and ready to go. Once this is done and the game is one that everyone has given two thumbs up to, then you are ready to do the advertising to bring in more people. You don't want to charge people money for a game that isn't finished or that has nothing to offer them.

Don't Give Up!

One of the biggest pieces of advice you should take is to stick with it. You can make sure that your game works out for the best as long as you stick with it and keep it going. Don't make the mistake of giving up on a game that shows promise. Adapt your game, make improvements and work hard to help it gain exposure and it should be successful over time.

All of those games that you love to play like Car Simulator, Bloxburg and others started out being small games but have grown over time because everyone loves to play them. That's a big win for those game developers and the players interested in the games as well.

MAKING ACTUAL MONEY ON ROBLOX FROM GAMES YOU MAKE

The biggest and best way to make money while on Roblox is to make games. If you can make games where thousands upon thousands of people come to play them, then you are a leader in the world of Roblox and making cash.

There are a few additional ways to make Robux while playing on Roblox, it's up to you to decide which options you like the best.

Asking People to Buy Access: This is one of the most popular ways to make some cash off of the game. When people come to play the game, you can ask them to gain access to the game with a small fee. It doesn't have to be too much to give them access to the game.

Many of the games that are in Roblox are free to play but it is not uncommon to come across games that do charge a small amount for you to gain access to play them.

MEGA BUILDER

Springtime Sabina
By ROBLOX

Price	(R$) 250
Type	Accessory | Hat
Genres	Adventure
Description	The truest symbol of a new season. Flowers bloom at the sound of her roar. Sabina.

Buy

Try On | 3D

☆ 638

Recommended Items

Snow Leopard	Holiday Crown	Stage Prop	Shade Samurai	Valentine's Day Cap	Eternal Top Hat	Straw Hat
By ROBLOX	By ROBLOX	By ROBLOX	By ROBLOX	By ROBLOX	By ROBLOX	By ROBLOX
150	50	100	55	350	150	98

Game Passes Offered: Having people come into the game to play but offering them the choice to purchase game passes that offer extras to the player. This type of option works a lot like the downloadable content that you can purchase from your console games.

These passes provide exclusive content or things that might help you win the game or make the game more enjoyable or enhance the game in some way. They are an optional pass that they can purchase since the game is free, they don't really need it to play, but it would be nice to have to play the game.

A lot of people prefer to have this option in many of the games.

Offering T-Shirts or Other Enhancing Items: When you have a game, you can set up a booth or a vending machine that provides a T-shirt or other item for the players that come into the game. It is almost like offering a souvenir at a shop. You are giving them something from the game for a small price. This is then transferred to your account when they purchase one.

This is an option that can now be done in the game making mode, so it is definitely an option that is worth it. You can add your little shop in just minutes, and it can bring in a serious amount of Robux if you get many players to your world.

ROBLOX

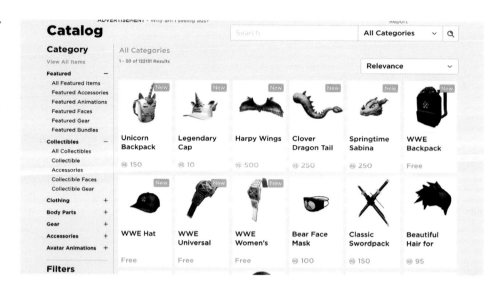

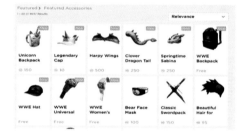

TRADING ITEMS FOR CASH

Another way to make money on Roblox is through the trading platform that they have. You can trade exclusive Limited Items on the system. This allows you to get new items and trade them for other items or make some cash from them.

Limited Items are rare to come by and they are worth a decent amount to the right player. The creators of Roblox have made these items and released them in a limited supply so they're rare and often very valuable. Usually there were only a few of them that were sold during a specific time period. If you purchased one of these items you can often sell it for a nice profit, and if you didn't, you'll have to resort to buying it from other players to gain access to it.

You can purchase the rare items from the trading platform. Other players are more than happy to offer the items to those that wish to purchase them for a specific set amount of Robux.

The trick with this is that you have to keep your eyes on the exclusive and limited items that come and go from the marketplace in the catalog. When these items come up, you are the one that decides whether or not they are going to be popular items. You want to purchase the items that you think are going to show promise and be more popular in the coming future. You can then offer them up on the marketplace to other players for purchase.

Relevance ⌄

MITED
ROBLOX
ladness
Vas 🔘 100
🔘 9,898

LIMITED U
Playful
Vampire
Was 🔘 75
🔘 6,399

LIMITED
Sinister
Branches
Was 🔘 125
🔘 2,500

LIMITED
The Classic
ROBLOX
Was 🔘 900
🔘 57,500

LIMITED U
Evil Skeptic
Was 🔘 50
🔘 21,212

LIMITED U
Radioactive
Beast Mode
Was 🔘 100
🔘 11,299

MITED | **LIMITED U** | **LIMITED U** | **LIMITED U** | **LIMITED U** | **LIMITED U**

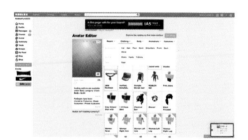

You can set the price for these rare items that other people are after because they are your items and you can ask whatever you want for them. They will then pay you in Robux and once you meet the requirements, you can cash them out for real cash.

CASHING OUT WITH ROBLOX TO CASH

If you have made a decent amount of Robux but you don't want to spend them in the game, then it might be time to exchange them to real-life cash. This is easier said than done because Roblox makes sure to put some rules and regulations on how you can cash out with this type of payment from their website.

Screenshots: Roblox® ™ & © 2019 Roblox Corporation

In order to cash out the money and meeting all of these requirements means you get $0.0035 per every 1 Robux you have. This means that you get $350 for every 100,000 Robux that you earn. This is a decent amount of money to cash in on, so it might be worth it to continue to collect until you meet all three of the requirements that are given for the player. The daily limits to cash this money out is over a million, so usually players do not have to worry about this unless you have an extremely high grossing game.

YOU EARN MORE IF YOU'RE IN THE ROBLOX BUILDERS CLUB

Everyone is able to sell access to the games that they make in Roblox. You can charge anything from 25 Robux to 250 Robux. Regardless of whether or not you have a Roblox Builders Club membership, you can still make Robux from the game that you make.

According to the website, in order to cash in the Robux for cash you have to meet all three of these requirements:

· You have to be 13 years old or older to cash it in

· You have to have a minimum of 100,000 Robux that you have earned in your account that you can cash in

· You have to be a member of the Outrageous Builders Club tier

Upgrade to Roblox Builders Club

	Free	Classic	Turbo	Outrageous
Daily Robux	No	R$15	R$35	R$60
Join Groups	5	10	20	100!
Create Groups	No	10	20	100!
Paid Access	10%	70%	70%	70%

	Monthly	Monthly	Monthly
	$5.95	$11.95	$19.95
	Annually	Annually	Annually

For billing and payment questions: info@roblox.com

Buy Robux

Robux is the virtual currency used in many of our online games. You can also use Robux for finding a great look for your avatar. Get cool gear to take into multiplayer battles. Buy Limited items to sell and trade. You'll need Robux to make it all happen. What are you waiting for?

Buy Robux

Buy Robux with

iTunes In-App Purchase

Those that do not have the membership however, have to pay a 90% fee on the Paid Access sales that they make through their game. All those that are in the Builders Club have only the 30% regular marketplace fee that is given. This is a big difference and one of the biggest reasons why people choose to get a membership.

This is because the makers of Roblox want to make sure that they limit the number of scammers that are in the game just to collect the Robux and not actually provide value through their games. This is something that can essentially be caught and then the game that is guilty of this can be removed from the server.

What does this mean for you?

Developer Exchange Terms of Use

Roblox Terms of Use

Roblox Privacy and Cookie Policy

Developer Exchange Terms of Use

Roblox Community Rules

Roblox Name and Logo Community Usage Guidelines

Thank you for your interest in the Roblox Developer Exchange Program (also known as DevEx). DevEx is a program that allows certain Roblox users to exchange earned Robux for real currency, as more fully described below.

1. Acceptance of Terms. Below are the terms and conditions that govern use of DevEx ("**DevEx Terms**"). These DevEx Terms are part of the Terms of Use, and the term "**Services**" shall have the meaning set out in those Terms. If you do not agree to those Terms, which includes these DevEx Terms, you may not participate in DevEx.

2. Eligibility Requirements to Cash Out. If you (a user of Roblox who is 13 years of age or older) both have at least 100,000 Robux in your account and are a member of the Outrageous Builders Club, you will be presented with an option to exchange your Robux for U.S. dollars at the then current exchange rate set by Roblox ("**Cash Out**"). Further information on how to Cash Out can be found at the DevEx help page.

3. Determination to Cash Out. Based on your account information, on the requirements below, and on applicable laws, we will make a determination in our sole discretion of whether you are eligible to Cash Out. Please note that (a) the maximum value for Cash

It means that if you are thinking about charging an amount for the entrance into your game, then you should make sure to provide a valuable, fun game that has content that people want and choose to play. This way, no one is missing out on being a great developer and actually getting the exposure and money they deserve. It also means that you should upgrade to a Builders Club membership once your game starts making Robux.

ROBLOX

Plus, we know you have some great games that you want to make up and show off and we believe you can do that without scamming people. Just make sure to watch out for the scammers yourself!

Additionally, those games that end up becoming quite popular on the platform have a separate section all their own that they are put into. This is known as the Top Paid section of the games and those games are placed on a sliding scale on the front page of the website.

Want to make the game that you made have paid access?

Just follow these simple steps:

Build page > **Configure** located under the **Gear Icon** under the drop-down menu > **Sell Game Access**

Keep in mind that there is a comment section that is located on the game. This is there so that other players that come in to play the games can let future players know more about the game before they decide to purchase access. It is almost like they are reviewing the games for everyone else to give them an idea.

This part of the game and monetizing what they are offering is not something that you can turn off. It is open to everyone and everyone is welcome to read the comments before they purchase so they know what they are purchasing beforehand.

QUICK TIPS FOR MAKING MONEY IN ROBLOX

Here is a list of some quick tips to take with you before you decide to make your own game. You can use them to your advantage and make the most of what they have to offer or what types of games you can make if you keep these tips in mind.

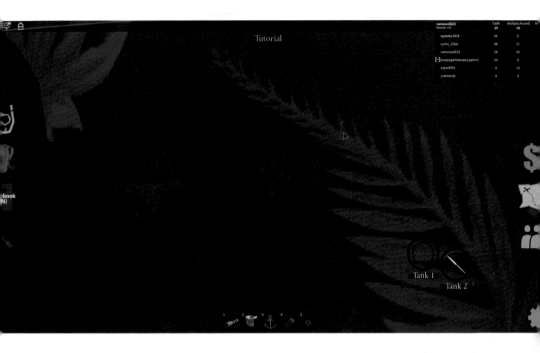

- Always make sure to remember that game play comes first, not making money. This might be hard to remember, but if you do, you can make an awesome game that does well.

- Give your players incentives to come back. You can offer free gear, loot crates, bonuses and more in the game.

- Know what people are buying in the game more than other items. This gives you an idea of what to charge for what items and which are more likely to be purchased.

- Build things for others that they request in your game whether it is gear or things that they want to have put in the game.

- Offer special game passes that not everyone has that gives them the ability to do something awesome in the game.

- Ask people! You need to make sure that you speak with people both online and around you. Knowing what your audience wants puts you in a great position to give them it.

There are so many different ways that you can make cash in Roblox that no specific strategy is the best one to follow. You don't have to worry about not being able to deliver an awesome game if you don't want to. There are many ways to make Roblox profitable to you whether you make a game, sell items or make items of your own.

Everyone has something that they like about Roblox and if you are looking to boost your efforts and really make some cash, it is possible to do just that. You just have to stick with it and you will get there!

![ROBLOX]

ROBLOX

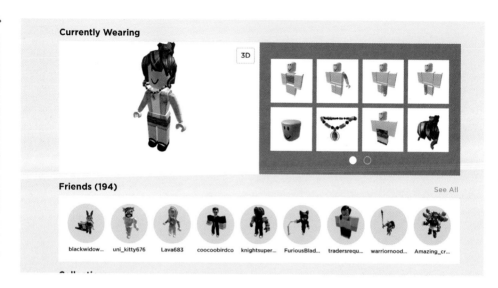

Earning Robux and Spending Robux

If you're thinking about becoming a part of the Builders Club, you will need to get Robux for this, as well!

We can give you more information about earning and spending Robux in the game. This is one of the biggest parts of the many different games that so many players enjoy. When you are able to take advantage of the currency system that the game offers, you can unlock special perks and features on most games that you encounter. A few Robux here and there can vastly improve your Roblox experience.

When you want to earn Robux, you need to know where to go to do so. This takes time to learn. Once you know how to generate Robux, you can start thinking about the many different ways to spend them from within the Roblox platform.

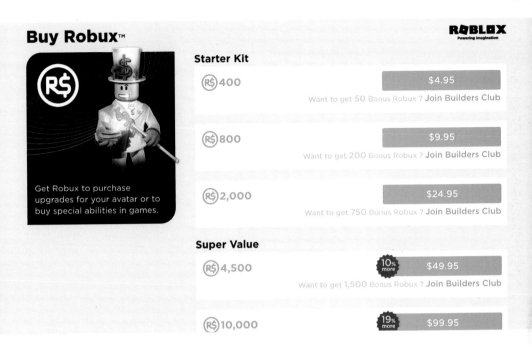

Buy Robux™

ROBLOX
Powering Imagination

Get Robux to purchase upgrades for your avatar or to buy special abilities in games.

Starter Kit

(R$) 400 — $4.95
Want to get 50 Bonus Robux ? **Join Builders Club**

(R$) 800 — $9.95
Want to get 200 Bonus Robux ? **Join Builders Club**

(R$) 2,000 — $24.95
Want to get 750 Bonus Robux ? **Join Builders Club**

Super Value

(R$) 4,500 — 10% more — $49.95
Want to get 1,500 Bonus Robux ? **Join Builders Club**

(R$) 10,000 — 19% more — $99.95

Learn more about the many Robux options that are available to you and other players out there.

Everyone loves a little money and when you're a Robloxian, you love a lotta Robux!

PURCHASING ROBUX

Purchasing Robux is something that you can do at any point in the game. You just have to go to your account. This is where you can buy and spend all of the Robux you want. However, to purchase any of the Robux, you need to make sure that your parent is okay with giving you the money for the game.

Your parent has to put in their credit card or other account information to purchase the Robux for you.

They can pay by Visa, Mastercard, Discover or American Express.

They can also use their Debit Card or PayPal Account.

If you have a Rixty or Roblox card, these can be put into the account for you to redeem as Robux.

Once you choose how much you want to purchase—the larger amounts give discounts—you can then cash out and use the added area to input all of the information that they ask for in order to pay for your purchase.

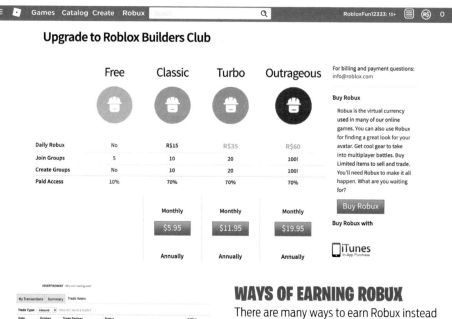

WAYS OF EARNING ROBUX

There are many ways to earn Robux instead of having to purchase them all the time. This is something that a lot of players don't think about. You might think it is going to take lots of time to really make anything, but you can make a decent amount in a short amount of time and then use the Robux in your account whenever you like.

Here are some of the ways that you can become a Robux earner right on the game, so you don't have to ask your parents to buy you a Robux stack.

One of the biggest ways to earn Robux in the game is through requesting people pay to get into the game that you have made. This is something that more and more creators in Roblox are now doing. In order to play the games, you can pay to gain access to it. Once you do, you're in and you get to keep playing.

They also ask if you want to add on Builders Club. You can choose the tier that you want, or just leave them unchecked if you just want the Robux and you do not want to add in the club with the purchase.

You can play the game without having to purchase Robux. You just are able to purchase more in each of the games, get access to the games or even customize your avatar more if you have Robux in your account. It's good to know how to obtain Robux if you want to access all the exclusive features in the games and to maximize your Roblox character.

The other way that has to do with game entrance fees is charging a VIP fee. Those that want to have full access to the game that they choose can pay to have this VIP standing. Usually they are given extras along with this status so that you can ensure that you're getting all that you need from the game.

These are not all of the ways that you can get money in the game though.

You can create a store to sell items for the game that you have made. This creates specialty items that you have created just for the game, such as hats and T-shirts that your fans of the game might want to purchase.

You can also provide a way for them to pay to use some of the features throughout the game, unless they are a VIP member, of course. If you didn't put a VIP fee or an entrance fee, then having them choose to open up special features throughout the game by paying for them is another option that you have in addition to selling the items that go along with the game.

Those that want to keep the making money part away from their game can do trading and selling in the catalog. If you are looking at selling rare items to others for cash, then you can do this, as well. This involves grabbing or finding those specialty items, rare items and other items that are only out for so long before everyone else does. Once you have them, you can trade and barter with others and even charge them to get the items from you.

If you like making the items and not so much the games, then you can make clothing items and other items and sell them in the marketplace catalog that everyone can look at. With pages and pages of items, you can make something specific and when people search for it, what you made can pop up on the page. These items are often easier to make, and you get 70% of the profit when they sell.

All of these methods are ways to make and earn Robux on the game. You can become as creative as you want when making and earning Robux throughout the game. Powered by kids, just like you, you can create a full-time job for yourself playing on here and you can even cash in on this money you have earned when you gain enough Robux because the game will transfer it back to you in actual cash.

If you don't want the cash or you are not making that much, then you have other ways to spend the Robux in the game and to enjoy your earnings.

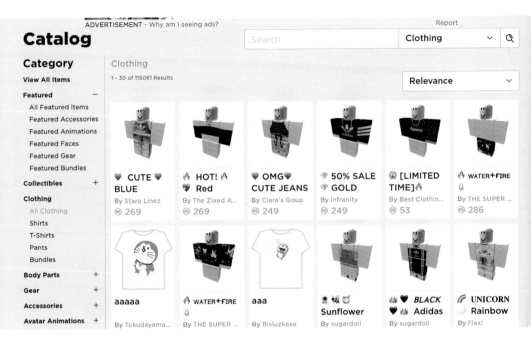

SPENDING ROBUX IN THE CATALOG

You probably already know how to spend your Robux once you have earned it. Everyone loves the spending part of getting money, don't they?

You're one of those people that love to grab a good thing when you have the money to do so. You can do that using the Robux that you earned from one of our methods up above.

We have created a section in this very book with many different catalog items that you can look at and buy for yourself and your character. With so many great options being offered, there is a bit of something for everyone.

Of course, we have to go over some of the awesome swag here too before covering the items more in-depth in the Catalog section because you definitely want to see what you can spend your Robux on while you are customizing and creating your character.

Korblox Mage

Want something awesome to wear? Want to look cool while you walk around in the many different places that you visit? This is the awesome suit that you can throw on and wear around town.

Silver Helmed Hero

The gold and silver come together to create one of the best helmets you have ever come across. With wings in the back and a shiny look, this is the helmet that is truly going to stand out no matter where you are in Roblox.

Penguin

This is pretty much exactly what it says it is. You can become a penguin when you throw this outfit on and waddle on out of here.

Neon Bombastic Animal Hoodie

Become an animal when you throw the hood on. It is colorful, bright and you will be sure to be spotted in just about any crowd that you walk through. Who said cool things couldn't be found in the catalog?

Violet Valkyrie

It is purple, it has feathers and it really makes you look like a royal victor in the world. It is a hat made only for winners.

Burger Launcher

Wanna launch some burgers? This is the tool that you are going to want to throw over your shoulder. Put it on and toss burgers out into hungry crowds everywhere you go. You'll be the VIP for sure with this gadget!

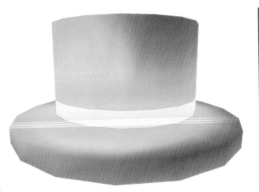

Blue Top Hat

Want to be at the top of the show with the best hat on? You can be sure to really make a grand entrance with this blue top hat. Blue not your color? They also have other colors, pink, orange, black and even purple.

Steampunk Hoverboard

You have the regular hoverboard and then you have the awesome steampunk version. This is definitely the one you are going to want to go with when you go to ride around town. Check out all the cool ratings this thing has.

Robot Guard Dog

Guard dogs are pretty awesome on their own and when they are robotic, they're pretty amazing! This is truly the dog that you want to have at your side. He is able to shoot lasers, which makes him even cooler and plus, you can remain protected at all times with him.

Tri-Laser 333

You want to protect yourself but maybe you want something that is pretty awesome to walk around with, too. You can check out this hand gun that provides the shooting power you need and the winning action you love. It shoots three lasers at any time, no need to reload.

Korblox Ice Dragon

You can get the most out of your transport with these ice dragons that are there to bring you to your destinations. Just pull them out and ride on them. Use the keys on the keypad to bring you around.

Beat Up Super Jank

This comes with the high ratings and an awesome set of sounds that you need. Everyone likes the tunes and even though this looks old and weathered, it is going to give you the beats that you need regardless of where you're playing them.

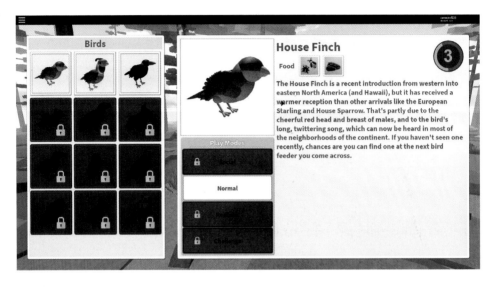

ROBLOX

Another excellent way to use Robux that you earn is putting it back into your business. You use most of the Robux that you earned in the game by trading and selling to purchase other rare items that you can trade and sell. This is how most stores work and operate and it is how you can do your business throughout the community, as well.

Of course, you can keep a little bit of what you made for yourself and spend it on something nice because all of that hard work has to pay off somehow! Just make sure to invest a lot of it back into your business!

SPENDING ROBUX IN GAME

So many people have been in the catalog looking at all of the things that they like and dislike and what they might want for their character, but there are other ways that you can spend your Robux when you are playing the game. This is something to think about if you have a lot of money left over from the selling that you are doing.

You can spend the money in any of the games that you go to play to improve your experience while in them. This can be everything from shirts to hats and anything in between. These items provide your character with something specialized to wear.

You can purchase VIP entrance into any of the games that you like that offers this option. You then are given all the access to all the special features available in the game. This is a great benefit that a bit of extra Robux can bring you.

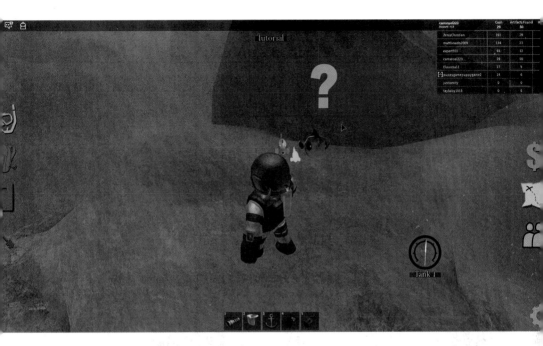

You can purchase access to any of the games that are out there. This is done using the Robux that are in your account. You can then enter the game and have access to it for as long as you would like to play it.

When you are in a game and they want you to pay to play a part of the game or to have access to something in a game that you are playing, you can do so if you have Robux to spend. This allows you to open up even more avenues in the game that you would not have been able to open up previously.

These are just some of the ways that you can come across spending the Robux in the game. You are likely to find many additional ways to spend the money as time moves forward and so many new features come out.

Spend your money in any way that you would like... it is your hard-earned money after all!

Upgrade to Roblox Builders Club

	Free	Classic	Turbo	Outrageous
Daily Robux	No	R$15	R$35	R$60
Join Groups	5	10	20	100!
Create Groups	No	10	20	100!
Paid Access	10%	70%	70%	70%

	Classic	Turbo	Outrageous
	Monthly	Monthly	Monthly
	$5.95	$11.95	$19.95
	Annually	Annually	Annually

For billing and payment questions:
info@roblox.com

Buy Robux

Robux is the virtual currency used in many of our online games. You can also use Robux for finding a great look for your avatar. Get cool gear to take into multiplayer battles. Buy Limited items to sell and trade. You'll need Robux to make it all happen. What are you waiting for?

Buy Robux

Buy Robux with

iTunes
In-App Purchase

BECOME A MEMBER OF THE BUILDERS CLUB

Deciding to become a member of the Builders Club is an exciting decision that can improve your gaming experience in Roblox. Before you can make this decision, you need to know what options are available to you though. There are three tiers and each of them provides something different to you. You wouldn't spend your money on something that you don't know much about, right?

We are here to give you that information to find out if the Builders Club is right for you.

FREE

The free account is what everyone starts off with when they enter into the world of Roblox. You do not get daily Robux to spend in the game and you cannot create groups or get a bonus. You get 10% of the paid access that you put on your games that you make.

CLASSIC - $5.95/Month

The next step up is the lowest club price that you can make use of. You get 10 groups to join, 10 groups you can create, and 15 Robux to spend, 100 Robux bonus and 70% of the access money that you charge guests.

Did you know?

If you are a member of the Builders Club, you are given a daily Robux stipend that you can spend in any way that you would like. This can get you into any of the games, providing you with VIP access, you can purchase cool items from the catalog, or you can save it so that you can buy something more expensive and even better!

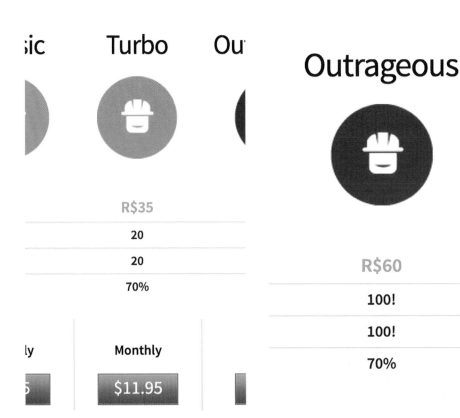

	sic	Turbo	Ou	Outrageous
		R$35		
		20		
		20		
		70%		R$60
				100!
				100!
				70%
	ly	Monthly		
	5	$11.95		

TURBO - $11.95/Month

The next step up, you can get 35 Robux to spend every day when you have this account and you get 20 groups to create, and 20 groups you can become a part of. 100 Robux are given as a bonus and 70% of the money that you charge your guests to your game.

OUTRAGEOUS - $19.95/Month

This is the biggest and best of the club that you can get. You get 60 Robux to spend every day on whatever you want, you get up to 100 groups you can create and 100 more you can become a part of. You also get the 100 Robux bonus for signing up and you get 70% of the money that you make from those that visit the game.

	Free	Classic	Turbo	Outrageous
Daily Robux	No	R$15	R$35	R$60
Join Groups	5	10	20	100!
Create Groups	No	10	20	100!
Paid Access	10%	70%	70%	70%

		Monthly	Monthly	Monthly
		$5.95	$11.95	$19.95

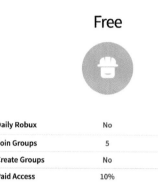

	Free			
		Monthly	Monthly	Monthly
		$5.95	$11.95	$19.95
		Annually	Annually	Annually
		$57.95	$85.95	$129.95
Ad Free	No	✓	✓	✓
Sell Stuff	No	✓	✓	✓
Virtual Hat	No	✓	✓	✓
Bonus Gear	No	✓	✓	✓
BC Beta Features	No	✓	✓	✓
Trade System	No	✓	✓	✓

If you are looking to become a part of the club, then you have all of these options to go with. You can choose which one works with you and what you want. Of course, the club is where it's at when you need to spend some daily Robux, grab extra bonuses and become part of awesome exclusive groups.

The Builders Club is a club that everyone is a part of, and it is definitely a club you want to be a part of if you play on Roblox frequently. Sign up whenever you want and get the most from your membership every day you play.

When you're ready to spend some of your hard-earned Robux, just know that you have plenty of different options to work with. The creators made this game to give players tons of options to work with, so they can be creative and play the way they want to. When you are a kid, this is your domain and you can become a creator, or you can just play.

With a community that has been built by kids, for kids, you are going to be able to fit right in with what they are providing you with, which is an ideal way to go about getting the most from the game.

Have fun while playing and know that Robux can be spent in any way that you deem necessary. If you want to get more items for your character or if you want to purchase items to sell, or if you want to play in any of the games that are asking for VIP access or just paid access into what they offer, then you have come to the right place.

With enough Robux available, the sky is really the limit as far as your spending options are concerned!

ROBLOX

In Other News

Roblox is shown in the news from time to time and when they are, you probably want to know what they are up to. Many of the stories from the company that brought us Roblox are great ones and worth listening to. Rarely do you hear of anything bad about this game because they are doing so much to make this a safe, fun area for kids and people in general to come in and have a good time.

Usually, if Roblox does show up in a news story, it's because the company is being praised for something exciting its doing.

Even if you missed these exciting stories when they were released, now you can look back and see those top news stories about your favorite game.

Roblox Launches an Education Initiative to Get Kids to Code

Coding is something that many kids are interested in, but many might not have the resources or even the push to learn how to acquire this cool skill.

That's why Roblox introduced a whole new education initiative for kids that want to code or kids that are learning how to code.

Education

Learn with Roblox

Roblox Announces a New Community Milestone in 2019

February 19, 2019 by Yoloylulu

COMMUNITY

one billion hours of engagement each month.

Roblox is a game that's all about bringing kids and teens together under one platform. Not only do the creators encourage children to test out the creations of others, but they encourage actively developing creations themselves as well. In other words, Roblox encourages kids and teens to learn how to code! Roblox is an excellent introduction to coding, but the company wanted to do even more for kids that want to code.

Some of these kids are extremely great at coding and they do deserve to be recognized as top coders in the game. When the Roblox community made note of this, the game makers decided that it would be cool to actively help push these gifted children to learn more about coding and to develop their skills further.

That's why Roblox Education was started. Roblox Education is their push to bring kids together with coding and to extend their creative muscle with a world that welcomes them to create and share their games with everyone. Whatever these gifted children can think up, they can do with the integrated Roblox Game creator tool.

ROBLOX

Educators

Roblox's creation tools and educational content are provided free-of-charge. As one of the fastest-growing resources for educators, Roblox allows anyone to build and publish their own games while learning real 21st century skills. Join our community of educators and ignite learning for millions of students worldwide.

Students

Anyone can build a game on Roblox. It doesn't matter if you're new to coding or you've never designed your own virtual world. With a little imagination and the right tools, you're already well on your way to taking the first leap into game development. Click below to start building your own worlds on Roblox today!

What Exactly is Roblox Education?

Roblox Education is a series of videos and tutorials that are aimed at providing coding help for those kids that want to learn how to make intricate games on the Roblox platform.

There are also other incentive programs that Roblox offers to those that come to play with them, not just Roblox Education.

Roblox offers summer internships to students that want to learn even more about coding and creating games. In addition to providing this educational tool, they want to be able to offer much more to those kids that use the gaming platform to create.

Many of the kids that are creating games within the platform are actually making a serious amount of money off of the games. This amount of money is a push to keep working hard and many of them have to learn money management skills as well after success with Roblox.

Roblox is actively fostering growth and knowledge by providing students with so many opportunities to expand on their knowledge of game making. They want to make sure that the kids interested that are already succeeding with their platform have a chance to do even better in the future.

Creative Commons License and Teachers

Educators that are teaching students coding or computer programming can use Roblox's tutorials, print outs, guides, step-by-step videos and more that teach students how to code on their platform with Lua.

For those teachers that are already teaching coding and other computer tasks, this is a great course to look into and use in their classroom. Many teachers have found the Roblox learning platform to be a useful tool for teaching children how to code. The best part is that it is a free learning program for teachers to use under the Creative Commons License.

Roblox also offers a cool set of summer camps that bring kids from all around the country to teach them how to code. In the program children are put in front of a section of computers to learn coding and to open up their minds and expand on their current abilities.

They also offer a free coding program for kids in partnership with Universal Studios. This is an initiative to get kids coding and make something unique along the lines of what the contest is asking. This is a great initiative for kids that want to build and expand upon their coding abilities even further.

Plus, Universal Studios is home to Jurassic Park and the last contest and coding program was themed after this movie series. The winners got free items in their inventory that they could use, such as a dinosaur, hat, shirt or other fun items. These are currently rare items that are being traded in the marketplace because only winners were the ones that got them.

ROBLOX

These programs are open up to any kids from around the world and they welcome those that have a creative knack and have already tried to build on the game, and they want to know how to bring their build even further.

Roblox Was Able to Raise $150 Million As Over 70 Million Players Visit

When it comes to the things Roblox can and cannot do, raising money was never something that they had to worry about. With so many players coming and going in the game, many of them gave to the game so that they could provide something bigger and better.

Many of the big hit games that are found on Roblox are user made and the players that created them were players that went through their free summer programs and camps to learn more. They want to find talent in the space and then foster this talent by showing them tips and tricks on how to make their games bigger and better.

This is definitely something to think about if you're a player developer within the game. Roblox can help you harness that creative side and build even bigger and better with the tools they offer. Even if you cannot make it to the camp or class, you can still benefit from the University section of the website that teaches you more through its tutorials and other guides.

The company was able to raise $150 million in order to expand their games reach further than ever before. This was a lot of money for one company to raise, but with the help of the players of the game, they made this a successful fundraiser.

Along with raising a massive amount of money, Roblox was also happy to announce that they surpassed the 70 million player mark. This is the number of monthly players that come into the game to play. This is not a total number of players that come and go from the system, but how many come into the game to play every month.

To generate the funding it needed, Roblox worked with Greylock Partners and Tiger Global Management, as well as the existing investors that were already putting money in the game and company, Altos Ventures, Meritech Captial Partners and Index Ventures. With the investment Roblox will make the game much bigger than Minecraft, surpassing the user amounts and the worth of the game.

With over 4 million players that are also creating games, there are currently over 40 million games available for new Roblox players to try out and have fun with.

Two of the players in the game that are top providers have more than one billion plays for the games that they have made. The hope is for many of the other players that are also creators to get the same types of outcomes.

ROBLOX

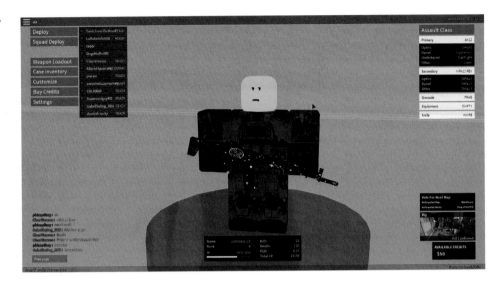

So, what is this money going to be used for?

The money that is raised is going to go to building out their infrastructure so that Roblox can handle a much larger base of players in the hopes that the game will continue to grow and expand. With a large number of players currently, thing have slowed down, and they need to expand in order to gain more traction on the interface.

The Roblox team also wants to provide more programs and abilities to the players and creators to help them make the most of their time with the game, as well as thinking about making an international move if possible. With so much growth happening inside the game, it is something that the developers are considering because they want to make Roblox available to everyone.

Roblox shares the revenue that they get from the games with the developers that make them. They feel that they should be rewarded for their hard work. With plenty of opportunities out there to make use of the Robux and the ability to turn it into actual cash, everyone is happy with all they can accomplish with the Roblox platform. Some kids have even managed to make a job from Roblox with enough practice and dedication!

The company continues to welcome new employees with 100 of them added over a year's time, they are continuing to see growth within the company and the game. They don't have any plans of slowing down and they have only accomplished a small portion of what they are looking to do in this game.

One of the biggest challenges is overcoming the filters and being able to put safety nets in place for the younger kids that come to play the game. These filters can make it easier to censor bad language and make the gaming environment more positive for everyone.

Roblox continues to grow and offers bigger and more exciting opportunities to the kids serving as creators on its platform. Even though there are some people that talk about how Roblox is unhelpful, the company does a lot to help children learn and succeed.

With the growth of electronics and technology, the need to know programming languages and coding is important. Lua, which is what Roblox uses, is one of the easier languages, but it is one that provides the user with many options.

Playing is fun when you're on the interface and whether you want to build or not, you have many different options and they provide you with all the information and training you need to create bigger and more exciting things if you want to succeed at a higher level. Everyone wants to be able to improve on their skills and with the use of Roblox, more kids are learning to program and design games than ever before.

The technological world is expanding more and more every year, and Roblox is a powerful tool that's helping children built on their creativity and learn important technical skills too.

RobloxFun12333 has joined the game.
rincessevabo has joined the game.
nny_thecat: ######

MEGA BUILDER

Cook
  Lillalinus12
Pizza Boxer
  masteradrian523
  Ginny_thecat
Delivery
  RobloxFun12333
Supplier
On Break
  vickyh2006
  jess74711
  xXCcaattssXx
  kaileyzoegtz
  THEK1LLABEAST
  princessevabo

Did You Know?

If you're looking at boosting your gaming brain power and learning more about your favorite game, then this is the section that you'll probably be most interested in. Here you can easily grab some tips, tricks and facts. Spend a bit of time reading through this section and you'll become the know-it-all of the Roblox world.

If you're ready to kick butt in the game of everything-you've-ever-wanted-to-know about Roblox, then you've come to the right place!

How many people play Roblox per month?

Around 80 million players play this game per month. The numbers continue to grow and many of these players come on during specific times throughout the day together. That's why you might experience some lag while playing at certain times.

How many people have downloaded Roblox?

Around 175 million downloads have been initiated of the game, though there might not be that many players actively playing.

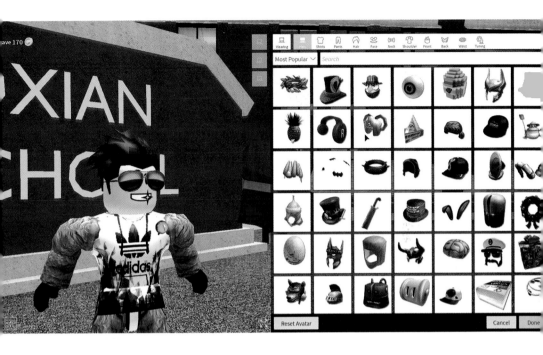

How many hours do kids play Roblox per month?

On average, close to 52 million hours have been spent playing Roblox by players on the game that are 13 or under!

How many players on Roblox are also creators?

4 million of the players that are on Roblox are also creators on the game. This means they play and create worlds that people visit.

How many employees work at Roblox and keep the game and servers running?

400 employees work at the office and provide the server with updates and other extras, including games and new item downloads.

ROBLOX

Race beginning in 15 seconds

CODES
REBIRTH
MARKET
TRAILS
CRATES

Level: 9
Exp: 23/28
Speed: 24
Races: 0
252

PETS
SPEEDY BAR
DIAMONDS

Join Speedster Studios to unlock the
Epic Face Trail

How much is Roblox worth?

Roblox is estimated to be worth $2.5 billion.

How many players at one time were playing on Roblox?

Currently, the most players that have been on the Roblox server at one time together was

1.7 million players.

How many Roblox items were made in 2018?

There were over 550 items

that were made and placed in the catalog in 2018 alone. The number is expected to be much higher for 2019.

How much time do kids over 13 play on Roblox per month?

Those that are under 17 but over 13 that play on Roblox spend close to **33 million hours per month** playing the game. This is not even close to the amount of time spent playing by those under the age of 13.

How many Roblox games were played in 2018?

Players went to over **34 billion games** that year, though many of them didn't get the top spots on the front page of the website.

ROBLOX

How many times is the website visited or viewed every month?

The Roblox website and its pages are visited close to **7 billion times per month.**

How much do the top Roblox games get every month?

It is estimated that these creators made around **$100,000 every month** off of their top earning game.

Which game on Roblox was the first to surpass the 1 million visitor mark?

MeepCity was the first to receive this status.

How many countries are players accepted to play in Roblox?

Over 40 countries are able to come on the website to play Roblox.

- **29 million in North America**
- **24 million in Europe**
- **16 million in Latin America**
- **14 million in Asia**

67% of the revenue that comes from mobile devices comes from North America alone and only small percentages come from the other countries playing the game online.

Can you play Roblox on more than just the computer?

You can play Roblox on many, many things. Whether you have a **Mac** or a **Windows PC,** you can play on both of these. You can also play on **Xbox One, iOS or Android** devices or even through the **Amazon App Store.** You have many options to play whether mobile or through the computer or on your gaming console.

ROBLOX

Is Roblox like Minecraft?

Your parents have probably asked you this or thought you were playing Minecraft when, **in fact, you were playing Roblox.**

While it does allow you to build like Minecraft does and create worlds that really stand out, Roblox is much more than what you'd get from Minecraft.

You can create games that you can actually play. You can create many more things and not everything is square shaped, which makes building a bit easier.

Minecraft is fun, but some of us players prefer Roblox because of the extras that it provides and opens up.

Do you have to get Robux?

While you don't have to get Robux, a lot of kids like to personalize their characters and really give them a great look. The money can also buy some of the coolest features in some of the games, so you can fit in or just do things other players without Robux are unable to do. **You can definitely do more with Robux, but you don't need them.**

Roblox is completely free, isn't it?

Some kids are worried about not being able to play the game with their friends because they don't have it. **Luckily, Roblox is free to play.** You just have to download the interface to the specific device that you are going to be using.

Once there, you can sign up for an account and sign right on. **You don't have to worry about paying for anything.** Some of the games and gear costs Robux, but you can still have access to many of the other parts of the games that are offered.

ROBLOX

Do you need space to download all of the games?

A lot of people ask if they need to have space on their computer to play all of the games that are on the interface that they want to play. **You don't.** You just have to click on them to play them and you can then **enjoy them without having to download them to your computer.**

Did you know that there is a Roblox University?

This is a series of videos that those kids that are serious about building games learn everything that they need to know to build their own. With tutorials, tips and more inside these videos, you just need a bit of time to go through them and find out all that they have to offer. It is definitely worth a look for those that want to play and get more from the games they make.

Did you know Roblox was going to add Pets?

Although there were rumors that Roblox was planning on adding special pets to the game, **the company decided not to in the end. Instead, they gave speed coils and other items instead of special pets that you could get that would give you special powers.** This was a bummer for some of us that would have liked to have that special pet with us while gaming.

ROBLOX

What does Roblox stand for?

It is actually a combination of Robots and Blocks that was put together. Playing into how the characters look and the making of the game, this makes the most sense because you are pretty much controlling a robot made of blocks.

Who do you think the youngest player of Roblox is?

Currently, the youngest known player on Roblox are three-year-olds.

How many hats can your character wear?

This might seem like a random question, but it is actually quite a cool one, especially for those that really love hats. **You can wear up to three!**

One of the most played games on Roblox is a capture the flag game, do you know it?

Ultimate Paintball is a popular game on the website. Made by Miked, this fun game provides all players with a way to get the flags and then bring them to the other side. Plus, there's plenty of places to hide along the way and paintball guns involved.

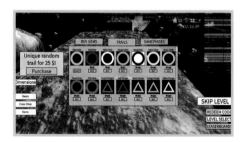

Do you know what R.S.S. stands for?

This is the Robloxian Secret Service group that is well known throughout Roblox. **They have around 40-50 members and in order to get in you have to be pretty cool.** There are numerous groups that you can be a part of when the time comes to enter into the world of Roblox and meet some new friends.

ROBLOX

If you are not in the Builders Club, you only get one place to build on

Those that are playing the game regularly and want to make a world for people to visit, whether it is one that is used for gaming or one that is just for visiting, you should keep in mind that you only get one because you're not in the club. **Get in the club and you are given more to build and play on.**

How many places do you visit in order to get the Builderman badge?

You can earn a lot of different badges when playing Roblox. Builderman badge is the one that so many players are going after. You have to build at least one thousand places though before you qualify for this badge.

The other badges that are out there also have qualifications that you have to meet in order to get them. You can check each of them out on your account section.

Some of the examples of the badges that they are offered include: **Homestead, Bloxxer, Combat Initiation, Veterans and others.**

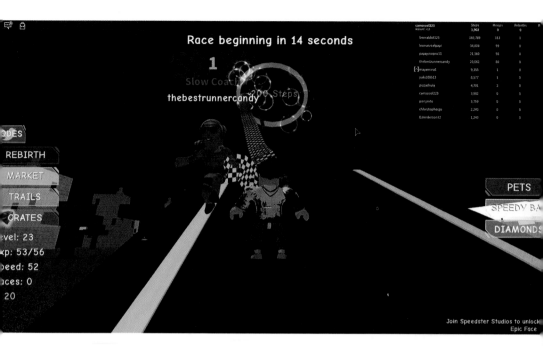

While these are just some trivia questions and answers and fun facts about Roblox, hopefully you know more about the game now than you did in the beginning. . You can visit the game for yourself and maybe come up with questions that might help you make a quiz all your own. This is a great thing to do, especially when you want to quiz your friends on everything they know about the game!

If you have learned at least one new thing by reading this section then we have completed our mission, but more than likely, you've learned a few different things and you'll probably have some more questions about the game and how it works after reading through this section.

Don't forget to spread the information to everyone you know and let them learn more about this game than they probably knew! ▪

ROBLOX

Safety Tips for Playing Roblox Online

Playing any game online, not just Roblox, calls for some safety tips and tricks that you need to keep in mind.

While your parents probably are looking in from time to time, it's important to make sure that you have the right safety information for playing this game. As fun as it might be, when playing online with other people you need to work to stay safe at all times.

What Roblox Has Done to Make the Game Safer

Roblox has heard the concerns of parents everywhere and because of this, they wanted to make sure that the game was safer for everyone, especially younger kids. This emphasis on safety occurred after Roblox characters began hacking into the game and exploiting other players.

There are now safety features that come with the game giving parents more control over their children on the game. They can choose which games kids have access to any time they are playing.

All Roblox players are split into two different categories. An over 13 section and an under 13 sections and players in the different categories have different rules and restrictions.

My Settings

Account Info

Security

Privacy

Billing

Notifications

2 Step Verification

Improve your account security. A code will be required when you login from a new device.

A verified email is required.

What are Account Controls?

You can setup account restrictions on this account to restrict access to account settings and uncurated content

Account PIN

Account PIN is currently disabled

Account Restrictions

Account Restrictions is currently disabled

This account can only access our curated content on the platform. Additionally, contact settings (under the Privacy page) will be set to Off.

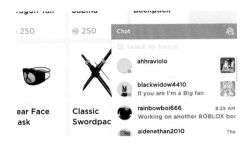

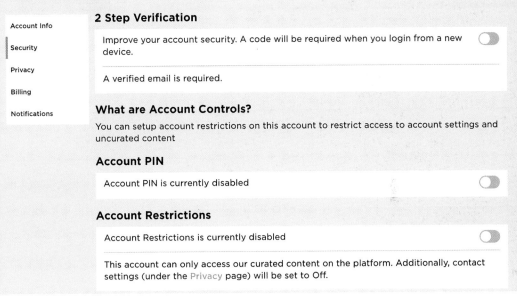

Chats and Privacy

The chats are one of the areas where privacy is definitely a concern. While it is important that kids are taught the proper online chat etiquette, sometimes this doesn't happen.

Due to this, Roblox decided to add a filter for younger children on the game. The filter removes all non age-appropriate phrases from the game to make it more enjoyable for everyone.

Not only that, but the players that are under this age are also stopped from providing personal information through their accounts. This is a good thing because you don't want to have them showcase this information.

It is important to note though, that sharing of personal information with any players regardless of age is prohibited anywhere in the game, so this is something to keep in mind. Personal information should be kept to yourself.

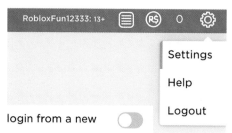

There is an indicator on the top corner of the screen that shows what type of account the player has. While this is not visible to other players, it is visible to the player that is on the account – 13+ or <13.

There are also further security features that can be customized by the player based on what they prefer to have done. You can limit or disable any of the features in the game such as the chat functions, the amount of information that is given out, who can chat with them or send them messages, as well as who can invite them to groups or games. Customizing this backend stuff is great for parents to do who have younger kids that are playing on Roblox.

How to Adjust the Chat Settings on a Child's Account

> Gear icon in the upper right > Settings
> Click Privacy > Privacy Settings Page
> Adjust the Contact Settings and Other Settings

> Players that are 12 and younger can select their Friends in the Game for Correspondence, or No One at All, those players over the age of 13 are given more options on who to speak with

Parents can also go into the **RESTRICTIONS** section of the game to set even more controls and security settings. They can even create their own **PIN** that allows them to sign in and keep control of the things the child is doing.

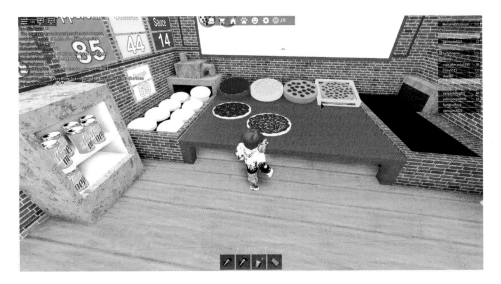

The PIN is used to make changes to the account settings. This means that once the parent puts a PIN in place nobody can go in and make changes to the settings made unless they know what the PIN is.

There are also HISTORY SECTIONS that grown-ups can look through when they sign into the account. You can go into the games, the chats, creations, friends and followers and many more options from this section. This allows parents to keep tabs on younger kids, what is being said by them and to them and anything else they are doing on the game.

You can even **BLOCK** users and **REPORT** them if they are abusing any of the rules that Roblox has set up for players. If they are harassing the other kids on the games, doing things that are against the rules and policies or anything else. This keeps the atmosphere safe and ensures that everyone is able to enjoy the game.

They want everyone to be able to use this feature if they notice something that is off or another player that might be bullying or harassing others. Don't let it happen. Don't watch it happen. Say something by reporting them.

ROBLOX

 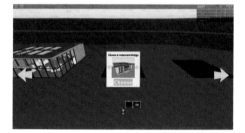

There is a way that you can do this right through your account. The players account also has an option for you to click to let moderators know more about the issue and why you are reporting that specific player.

Safety Tips for Those Playing Roblox

There are many other safety tips that players should be aware of while they are playing this game. Safety should be a top priority for any Roblox player. Using good safety practices will help improve your experience and the experience of other players as well.

Learn more about the safety options, rules and regulations you should keep in mind while playing on Roblox, or any other online game where you might meet new people.

- Never, ever give out any of your personal information like your whole name, your specific age, where you live – city, town, state, specific address, your phone number, your email or anything else that helps people online find you easier.

- If you come across a rude person or someone saying unacceptable things, then you can report them to the team by clicking the report button.

- Do not fall for scams and make sure to watch out for them. If people are asking you for Robux, for your account information, for items or anything else in return for something, do not accept or give them any information. You do not want them to hack into your account or steal your Rubux.

- Do not ask people on Roblox to be your girlfriend or boyfriend. Roblox has strict rules against this. Being friends is okay but trying to be more than that is not okay.

- Don't build anything that would harm players or hurt their feelings when you are putting it together. Try to be respectful of everyone and all players that you come across.

- Do not say bad words or curse at anyone in the game. You don't want to be reported for this and chances are, if you do any of these things, you are going to be reported for them. You might get banned.

ROBLOX

· Do not be gross or inappropriate with anything that you do in the game. This, again, can have your account banned if you are found to have done something like this.

· **DON'T SHARE PASSWORDS – EVER!**
This is a big thing that you need to think about because you don't want to share this information with anyone that might use it to steal your account. Don't give anyone access to your account but your parents!

· Do not spawn-kill people as they come into the game. You want to make sure that they are able to enjoy the game, get a second to get to where they are going and play. Killing them as soon as they spawn is not a good thing and it will never be a good thing. They can report you for this and they are not going to want to come back into the game because of how upsetting this is.

· Do not play any games that ask you for your account information to get hats or special products, they just want to hack you.

· If you're being bullied, block them and leave the game for now.

Whether your parents have told you these precautions or not, they are always important to follow. Roblox wants to make sure that the platform can stay open and the only way that this is possible is through the safest gaming techniques possible.

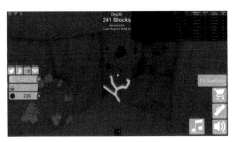

If you are thinking about some of the other ways that you can stay safe, then share them with your friends that play Roblox – or share the ones we have told you here with them!

Keeping everyone safe from those that might not be there for the fun is the best thing to do. You want to have a good time, but you want to make sure that those that don't belong don't get any information that you don't want them to have.

We are all here to keep one another safe. If you notice something that doesn't seem right or if someone approaches you and seems off, weird or is asking personal questions, you don't have to answer them, and you shouldn't have to. You should let Roblox know as soon as possible.

You are in control while playing this game. Just make the smartest decisions and you will be fine to play in any and all of the games that other players have made. You're welcome to join in and have fun, but by knowing those safety techniques you can really make sure that you're ready to have fun while making new online friends.

ROBLOX

Advanced Tips, Tricks and Hacks

While every game that you play inside Roblox is different and comes from a different developer, there are so many tips, tricks and hacks available that you can improve your experience in most games available with enough reading.

The top developers let us know important tips and tricks to help avoid common problems and improve the gaming experience each time we sign on.

The top players have sought after these tips and tricks, and use them on a regular basis. They even built their own games just to learn more about how Roblox works and to improve the gaming experience for everyone else and to provide useful building tips for others. Unlike some of the others out there, they want to make sure that other kids are able to come on to Roblox and build some games like they did.

So, what are these pros saying to players like us that just want some useful information to use?

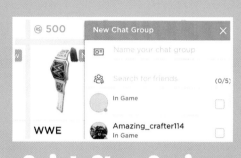

Quick Chat Option

Instead of trying to find the chat box and how everyone is chatting, all you have to do is click "/" and then type what you want into the box and click "Enter".

There is a bar at the bottom of the screen and if you play Roblox in Full Screen Mode, it makes things much easier.

Glitches Happen, Here are Tips to Deal with Them

When the game freezes, this can be very frustrating to deal with. Luckily, there is a way unfreeze the game, so you can get back to playing easily.

Press (CTRL) (F1) at the same time during game play.

This simple tip should help you solve most glitch issues as you play.

Spreading the Word on a Roblox Game

If you're an ambassador in the game, then you want to make sure that people know more about you and the group that you run. This means creating a website. However, blogs are much easier to run and deal with. You can have more time to play and less time dealing with a website and the ins and outs that go with it. Plus, a blog still looks as nice and gets the information across.

ROBLOX

Cool Dance Moves!

Want to do the moonwalk in the game?

That's easy enough!

Just press the (UP arrow) and (S) and your character is able to do a little moonwalking.

Giving Tips and Doing the Conversion

You can tip in the game, but do you know how much to tip?

You can use tradecurrency to get Robux when you type in the amount that you have. It automatically provides you with the amount that you get for the amount of cash you're putting into your account. It's pretty easy!

Did you know?

You can only play for 45 minutes in a game and then they kick you out? They want to make sure that popular games that many people are interested in have a space for everyone waiting. Don't let this upset you. Instead, try to see it as an opportunity to take a break from the game, or to test out a different game.

Enter Those VIP Rooms for FREE!

Everyone wants to be a somebody, even on Roblox and heading to the VIP room is the surest way to make you feel important. Did you know, you can actually enter the VIP rooms for free?

This quick trick works for many VIP rooms throughout Roblox.

Once you're in the desired game you just zoom in all the way on the screen. If there is a crack on the wall, then you just have to walk towards it. This will let you in the room, even if it is made for VIPs.

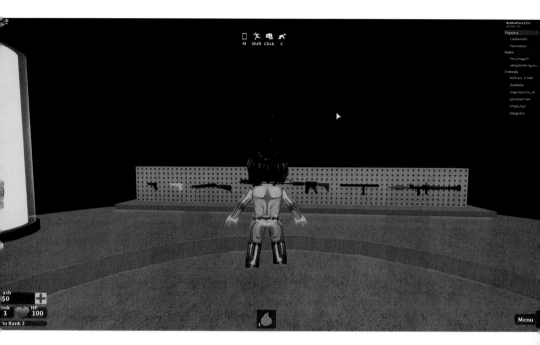

Fuse Weapons Together to Create New Weapons

Go to a game that has swords or other weapons, Telamon is a good one that many players like to go to, and grab two of the in-game weapons.

The key with this trick is that you have to have the right timing in order to do it. You just need to add these two weapons to your number bar, make one of them #1 and the other #2. Then you want to click on #1 and quickly follow that up with #2.

It might take a few tries to make it happen, but when you get the right timing you can actually fuse together your weapons to create a super weapon!

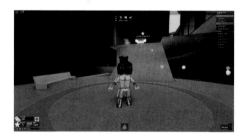

You can fight other players with your fused swords and it might triple the damage, but keep in mind that by doing this it might lag the game, so you will not have much time to escape when you are in the middle of a battle.

Make Backups

Always, we mean, always create a backup of your place when you are playing because Roblox Studio crashes!

Builders Club Tricks and Tips

Everyone likes to have a bit extra while playing a game online, and you can get even more out of the Builders Club using a few of our simple tricks. We know some codes and simple tricks to help you maximize your club experience.

Want to know the secrets?

Here they are!

Once you are in the Builders Club, you want to then type in "brickmaster5643" and they give you an extra 400 Robux into your account, just for typing that code in!

Want free OBC?

You can get that while in the Builders Club just by typing 94063 into the code box on the page.

Want to alter your level while playing, which will completely change the way you experience the game? Type / or use the – button and then enter 850000000000.

Want to rock a cracked ninja's mask? You might have seen them on other players and you can have the same mask, too!

Just get a round or perfection head and then wear it with the ninja mask. This creates the look automatically on its own.

You can actually do this with a lot of things that you put on your head. A paper bag is another item that you can put on your head and it shows that it is ripped.

Want to become a part of Robloxiaville's super VIP club?

It is much simpler than you think. All you have to do is go and purchase a Driver's License for a few Robux and wear it into the game. You're then in with the VIP crowd. Easy!

If you're not new to the game but there are many beginners that come in every single day. Want to trap them and let them know a bit about how the game works?

All you have to do is get an ordinary chair and turn it face down and then have the beginner sit in it. They are then stuck to it. Just don't go doing this to everyone because it can become mean after a while and your account might get banned if they tell on you.

Everyone likes a little zombie action and you can create your own zombie riot with a single zombie if you know what to do. You just need to click on the one zombie and then on the copier and delete tool. You've then made a zombie riot.

Your avatar's arms are able to go through any sort of bricks that you come across. Keep this in mind while in certain games that might seem like they trap you. However, there are exceptions to this rule. You cannot put your arms through lava blocks or killbots.

Want to get some points and have a laugh?

Just reset the stairs in the games and watch as the bodies coming through land in the teleporter instead of on the stairs they are supposed to land on.

Want to create the matrix?
This is something a lot of players have come across but not many players know how to create one – and creating one is pretty cool because you can call it your own matrix.

You just need 10 ghosts or zombies, more or a little less is fine but having 10 is ideal. You have to have a run tool around you. This tool should cause a lag in the game to happen. You then use the run tool and jump. This creates a matrix to get through.

Ever wanted to beat the invisible path game?

We have a solution on how you might be able to get through and ace it.

Use the green disc and place it over the edge, then bring it back to your character. From there, you shouldn't have any worries about losing this game, you have it under control!

Want More Roblox Fun and Perhaps Some Robux?

If you want to get a bit of fun and some Robux then you just have to visit Superkittyninja's place a few different times.

You have to visit exactly 16 times in order to get the benefits of being at this world. Go to the top of the mountain and jump twice while also pressing the F2 button. Then go to Roblox's crossroads and press F2 then leave the game.

Now press the F2 function and visit Superkittyninja's place once again. You are then given 4 Robux for your troubles. You can do this as many times as you want. You just have to go through the steps each time. Make sure to press F2 when you are done.

If you want to become invisible, which we are sure we all want to do at some point in our life, then give this cool trick a try!

Obtain a Witch Wand, use the green spray attack that is located on your action bar and then run into it. You will then be invisible in the game.

Have you seen the other players riding around on their flying toilets and want to make sure that you can do the same?

ROBLOX

Here are the directions to help you build your own flying toilet.

Place two cubed bricks on top of one another, jump on them and then place a toilet on the blocks. Then you have to remove the bottom brick from under the toilet. Place a floor lamp in your character and then sit down on the toilet.

Controlling the toilet is easy. You just have to press the space bar and use the arrow keys to move around. If you stop moving around, the toilet is going to fall to the ground.

Get a Flying Hat in Any of the Games You Play

You just have to be wearing a hat when you go into any of the games that are out there. Once in the game, just push the = button. You don't have to do any talking, just press the button and you're off.

Pressing this button in the game is going to cause your hat to shoot straight off your head!

Want the hat back?

It doesn't just come back to you, this isn't Mario Odyssey. You have to walk on it or die in the game to have it regenerated back on your head.

Fly on Things Other Than Planes

If you want to go for a little ride, but don't want to fly on a plane and actually have something else handy, like your skateboard, you're able to fly that around to wherever you want to go!

Go to the plane tool > insert a skateboard > ride the skateboard > use the plane tool to fly it like you would with a plane in the game

Go to the plane tool > insert a mini tank into the area > drive off of the base and it automatically floats in the air

You can also use the glitch that makes you fly You just have to put a 2x2, 2x3 or 2x4 brick on top of your avatar's feet and then one under your stomach and you're able to lift off!

Some Cool Tips Per Game

Do you play specific games and want an idea of what you can do inside them? We have come up with some pretty cool tips and tricks for some of the games out there.

Jailbreak

USE THE TASER! This seems pretty obvious, but you'd be surprised at how many people don't use it or fail to realize that they can use it.

USE THE GLIDER! This is great if you need to be somewhere fast and especially if you are located at the top of the tower. You can also use this if you are a prisoner at the jail and want to get away from the cops quickly.

SHOOT AT THE CRIMINAL to get them down, but don't kill them. There are speed hackers in this game that will try to run away pretty quickly. You can shoot them to kill them just to stop them because they will get away anyway.

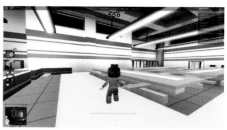

DON'T ROB A BANK: Rob something else if you want to try to get away with it. The cops usually catch people pretty quickly when you rob banks. Focus on easier targets instead, or proceed with robbing banks if you want a tough challenge! Also adjust the time you do the robbing to improve your chances.

GET A DONUT: These are going to be your 'get out of jail free' card. They can be used to persuade cops into doing things, letting you go or even helping yourself when you get shot by them. With so many uses, you are going to want to have a donut.

Retail Tycoon

This is a great game to play that is fun and there are a lot of beginner's tips that even the most seasoned players didn't know about.

Place two cash registers next to each other so that they form a square. If you stand in the middle of them, you can run both at the same time. This saves time, money and gets your customers out much faster. Plus, you don't have to hire anyone!

It's recommended that you buy the registers you run at first and not the self-checkout ones. You want to upgrade to those later on when you get going.

Want to change the songs that are playing in the background?

You have the option to do this too!

Just go to the Roblox shop and select the song that you want to play in the shop. Just make sure to look at the numbers or ID of the song because this is how it is identified. If you are looking for a specific song to play then you need to know the ID, which you can look up.

Tips and tricks are something that come with each of the games. Many players spend hours in games without learning about all the features and tricks available to them. Only the developers of the games know exactly what you can do and about little hidden tricks, but players discover them over time and we want to pass them on to you!

Take some time to go through those favorite games of yours to find out if you can find some of these hidden treasures within them.

ROBLOX

Building Hacks and Tricks

While some of these tips and tricks are something you should already know, it is good to go over some basics.

These are just quick tidbits to keep in mind when you go to make your own world.

- Always use the right tools for the job or task you are trying to accomplish.

- You can change the colors to make your world look more life-like if you choose. You don't have to because you can keep the colorful and blocky appearance if that's what you prefer, but just know that you have different color options available to you.

- Lighting is also going to make a difference. With the right lighting you can make it look like an overcast scene, a foggy one, a bright sunny day and so much more. Regardless of what anyone tells you, lighting does make a difference.

Useful Building Plugin!

All of these plugins are extremely helpful when it comes to adding more to your game and being able to create the look and feel that you need and want from your game.

Oozle Draw is one of the best to use when you want to smooth out those jagged lines and really give your world a life of its own. It will take a bit to get used to all of the options and tools this plugin has, but it can really make your world look and feel more professional than what the Roblox Builder gives alone.

You can check online for many tutorials that are in-depth on this awesome Roblox Builder plugin that many high-end developers use.

ROBLOX

Hacks and Cheats

Keep in mind that there are some videos and information out there about "jailbreaking" or "hacking" into Roblox. This is just a fancy way of saying getting more from the game than you are supposed to through exploits. You don't want to do this, because if you do get into the server then this is actually illegal and can get you banned, so don't listen to what they have to say about this and stick with regular game play and game making.

We've also noticed a lot of "cheats" that have been going around. Many of these I found do not work and many of them take away from the fun of the game. Some even kicked me off the server! Instead of having to deal with all of this, you should just skip this type of cheat and go right for those tips and tricks, and even those shortcuts that allow you to still have a good time without kicking other players off or leading to you being kicked.

If you have gotten pretty far into making your own game and world, then it might be time to think about entering into Roblox Education or Roblox University.

Find out how much more you can make and how much further you can go with a little help in the coding department. If you become really good, the makers of Roblox might just invite you out to do a camp or internship class with them. That would be pretty awesome, wouldn't it?

Know all of the tips, tricks and hacks and keep a few of your own up your sleeve and you just might become the best builder that the game has ever seen!

And, as always, make sure to check the Robloxia news often!

!? Help

⚙ Settings

$$ Buy Cash

Roblox: Behind the Scenes

Ever want to know what happens behind the scenes to really make Roblox tick?

Want to know what to expect when you are a big shot in their corporate offices or when you're a developer full time for the company?

Hey, you can dream, can't you?

Here is some information that can really give you a look straight into the heart of Roblox, whether you want to work there or not It's still interesting for you to know how much time goes into the work on the game and all the things that happen behind the scenes that a lot of players do not know about.

Here is some information about what is happening, the people that work there and of course, some behind the scenes looks into the offices where they work.

Roblox is located in San Mateo, California. So, they are in the sunny state of Cali and sometimes some of the developers and players are invited to come out and take a look at all that they do behind the scenes in real life.

At Roblox they hold classes and camps in these offices where they teach some of the top developers and players how to code better. They offer this training so that they are able to create better games and build a stronger community.

"Today, in any given month, we have about 3.3 million people playing on Roblox every month"

— David Baszucki, Founder of Roblox

Roblox got started as a game only with a couple people that were working together to build the website and trying to make it possible. They started small and worked to change their idea into something bigger and exciting. They have since grown to hire hundreds of employees.

They are working on making the platform safe and ideal for players aged 3+ that want to come in and have a good time. Want to check out some of the most awesome spots of the office and taking a nice little stroll through the hallways of the office?

Upon Entering

Upon entering the office, you'll see some of the coolest Roblox signs out there. This is what really makes the area stand out. That and the awesome sitting areas that they have to offer. You can enjoy lounging around if you don't want to go in and do some work, but most of the employees don't spend too much time in the lobby area.

While at the studio you'll also have a chance to look at some of the coolest toys ever created for Roblox. This is one of the coolest points in the hallway because they have glass cases full of toys that show off the players, the workers and the things you can find inside the game.

Another pretty cool thing that they have on showcase is the large flat screen television that is mounted up on the wall. This television is not just a plain one that has a show on it or that shows the game, but it actually shows a globe and all of the players that are signed into the game at one time. You can then zoom into the specific areas to find out what people are playing and the number.

This allows them to show off just how many players enjoy Roblox at any given point in time. Even while they are not at the office, this screen is able to take count of all of the players that are coming and going at any point in time.

ROBLOX

"We need to move offices, I want to work for Roblox now"

— PrestonPlayz, YouTuber in Roblox HQ, San Francisco, during his trip to the offices

Loads and Loads of Food!

If you love food, then the Roblox headquarters is where you want to be and where you want to work. You'll have immediate access to all of the drawers and drawers of food that they have in the shelves, the drawers, the fridge and freezer. Everyone is welcome to have some, whoever is working there. Roblox maintains an open kitchen, so everyone can eat what they like while there.

This is probably the best part because everyone likes food and if you are working for an awesome company, like Roblox, then you know that food is part of the deal.

If you love food, then so does the Roblox headquarters. All the food available will certainly be one of the highlights of your visit.

Make a Wish

Another awesome thing to know about Roblox and who they let in their headquarters is that they always do a Make a Wish event when they are asked to. The whole Roblox team understands the value of charity, and they can't help but work to make children's dreams come true. In addition to providing a learning experience, camps and classes for young coders, they make sure that when kids ask to meet them and go to their headquarters that they grant their wishes when possible because this is something that means a lot to the company and to the children.

All the extra stuff that Roblox does for children and for the community just shows that they care, and it's something to celebrate too. Roblox is committed to children, and it's an organization that can help them achieve their dreams too. That's one thing that helps separate Roblox from other organizations.

Awesome Coder Classes

The headquarters welcomes a handful of kids to come in and have classes or do a camp, for free, with their offices. They then show these kids some advanced coding skills and more that they would not be able to learn anywhere else.

"Do you know where the Golden Dominus is?"

— iifnatik, YouTuber in Roblox HQ, during his trip to the offices

How do they choose these kids?

They choose them through the developing section of Roblox itself. If the kids are making some of the best games that are showing high amounts of traffic and they are getting positive results, then they are going to want to harness that creativity and help them build a bigger, better game that really hits home.

They bring the kids into the office and put them through a coding boot camp where they can meet with the professional developers and coders for the game. This is an awesome opportunity and definitely one that you should feel privileged about if you are asked to come out and take part in this.

"This is the very first mockup of Roblox, we called it DynaBlocks at the time"

— David Baszucki, Founder of Roblox

Games are Played Behind the Scenes

When it comes to the employees behind the scenes at Roblox, don't worry about not being able to get in some game time. Workers are given plenty of time to play games throughout the day.

Playing these games is part of the job, because you don't want to worry about not being able to have the fun that comes with game time, especially if you are a backend employee with one of the biggest and best places out there to work!

What Exactly is it Like to Work at Roblox?

Many people, even us players that play the game, want to know what it is like to work at Roblox. If you ever plan on working at the company yourself, it's important to know what you can expect.

Rated highly by current employees working there, they make Roblox Headquarters sound like it is one of the best places to work. Not only is the atmosphere nice, but so are the perks, but we have already told you about the awesome looking office and the endless supply of food that they bring – they have even had a guacamole table at one point. That's not all that makes this job stand out though.

In the matter of how people are treated, everyone is treated fairly, and they make sure to make the workplace fun. The Roblox corporate leaders want to make this one of the best places to work and when you are in sunny California, then you know you're in the best place to work, both inside and outside of the building.

Roblox even takes in interns from other states to give them a chance to spend time around the office. However, getting one of these spots is definitely hard. If you're willing to put in the time and the effort, you can land yourself a spot at Roblox and enjoy all the different perks offered. Not only that, but if you are one of the kids that shows promise when you grow up playing and creating on the game, then you have a better chance of being noticed by the game developers.

Just make sure to keep creating because if you can get an internship at this office, then you'll build on experiences and gain insight and skills you can show off on your resume! Plus, we are confident that you you'll learn a lot at your time at the headquarters.

ROBLOX

"The first version of Roblox was simplistic and we made the first games, but decided that the games needed to be made by the users"

— David Baszucki, Founder of Roblox

There is a lot that goes on in these offices and a lot of times they have special events and other things happening to enjoy. We were lucky enough to be given the look inside the office, so we can tell you all about our unique experience.

Also, if you find yourself in San Mateo, they might just be putting on tours of the offices. Make sure to check the local newspapers and events information centers to find out if this is something available to you when you visit.

Take a tour through the facilities, or just watch others workers and other gamers experiencing some of the latest games on Roblox.

We've compiled a list of their names and we can show you where to find them if you want to watch some of the most awesome Roblox videos available today. They are entertaining and well worth a look.

Who Plays Roblox on YouTube?

YouTube is one of the most popular ways to watch other gamers connect with games they love. Want to know who is playing Roblox on YouTube?

You probably already know some pretty cool people. However, we are going to cover some of the best known out there and the ones that have a decent amount of views on the videos that they put up of them playing on this well-known game.

Here are some of those players... and please, share some of the others that you know on Roblox! It is always good to spread the word on your favorite YouTubers, especially those that are spreading the word about Roblox.

"I'm just causing problems ever since we showed up at Roblox"

— PrestonPlayz, YouTuber in Roblox HQ, San Francisco, during his trip to the offices

Hyper: Master of destruction and sneaky tricks, Hyper is one Roblox player that knows how to go unnoticed. In one of his top-producing movies he hides in his sister's Roblox home for quite some time before she even notices that he is there. As he is trying to move around the house and show everyone just how great she has built it, he is also spending time in other popular Roblox games on the same video. Hyper is an awesome player and an awesome YouTuber to check out.

GamingWithJen: She loves playing many different games, but she prefers games like Roblox where she can play alongside other players. Plus these popular games don't hurt her views! She is funny, and is able to show us a whole different side of Roblox that you might not have ever seen. With her funny talk and her fun antics, this is definitely a place for you to spend your time. Take a moment to stop by and see her videos, so you can get some great ideas! If you are into girl gamers, then she is definitely

ItsFunneh: Her videos are funny, and they provide the user with a way to look into the many games and areas of Roblox that you might not have known about before. The elevator video is one of the videos that has the most views. If you want to know more about Roblox and all that comes with being a player in the game, she will give you some insight. Plus, she can show you some cool customization tricks that come with having an avatar. She is a little less well-known than others on this list, but she also makes some of the best videos you'll find on YouTube with a focus on Roblox.

The Toy Heroes: As one of the best YouTubers that you can come across, especially since they do more than games. This group of YouTubers provide a unique look into the games found throughout the Roblox platform. They have a bunch of fun videos to watch, and some of their most popular videos showcase Roblox worlds you've probably been in yourself. It is definitely worth a view to see what they have going on. This channel's videos are also known because they are not just videos, they are entertainment at its finest.

ROBLOX

"I'm going to go inside of here and dab, okay?"

— PrestonPlayz, YouTuber in Roblox HQ, San Francisco, during his trip to the offices

FGTeeV: This is one of the most well-known YouTubers out there focused around children and Roblox. With fun around every corner, they have so many videos that you can watch of the family doing so many things. However, gaming is definitely something that they do and Roblox is one of those games that they have a good time on. If you search through their videos, you're easily able to find some that focus on Roblox in the middle of the others.

One of the biggest things we love about FGTeeV is that they include the whole family and you don't have to watch them play Roblox if you don't want. Their Roblox videos are something special though, and the kids really kick butt in many of the videos that they're playing Roblox games in.

ObliviousHD: As one of the most exciting YouTubers out there, you can expect to find that they have some more of the exciting videos that they made with Roblox that are turned into actual movies. This is definitely something that is going to stand out when you are looking into all that they can do. If you love Roblox, then you are going to love the videos that they have put together for their audiences. It is Roblox meets Universal Studios, which is pretty awesome and definitely something to think about and look into. A movie, a YouTube channel, and awesome Roblox player come together to provide an awesome mix to watch.

Jelly: Jelly is a pretty awesome YouTuber with Roblox aside, but having him play online with his girlfriend, they build some of the best things. You can put them together and watch as they create a new world. One of their last videos that got 1 million views was when his girlfriend built him a serious mansion in Roblox. Jelly is the one you want to check out for the information on how to build some of the best things out there.

Jelly is less known, but he is definitely one that provides some value, more so for older kids than the younger crowd. He still offers some insight into Roblox though and he invites some of the other well-known players to come into his

"In the beginning we knew every single person on Roblox, imagine that"

— PrestonPlayz, YouTuber in Roblox HQ, San Francisco, during his trip to the offices

TOFUU: The Tofuu that is out there is the Tofuu that you want to watch on YouTube. He is pretty much known for the awesome videos that he puts together and shows off. With awesome graphics and even better action, you can find exactly what you want. Just make sure to grab the popcorn and take a seat because when you're watching his stuff, it is pretty cool to watch, and he definitely has a lot of action jumps and places you are going to want to go and play for yourself on Roblox. He is just testing them out first for you.

ROBLOX: We are not going to keep this video section going without putting a nice shout out to Roblox themselves because they have a YouTube channel and account that you can be sure to make use of when you are trying to learn more about upcoming events, look at past events, or just check out some of the new upgrades and extras coming up. If you're ready for some more information, then this is your one-stop-shop to find it all out.

You can learn a lot watching the different videos put together by Roblox YouTubers. They'll give you a look into different worlds, and you can get ideas to put into your own world creations as well.

You can even become a YouTuber showing off the Roblox creations and avatar that you have! Start recording and showing off your gaming skills today to find out just how big you can get! It is well worth it, and there's nothing like showing off your videos to your friends.

Whether you are thinking about going to the office, or if you wanted to know what it is like to be a developer at the Roblox headquarters, hopefully this section answered some of those questions. Take a look at some of those YouTubers and start planning your trip to the Roblox headquarters yourself.

No matter what you want from a game, whether you want to create or be entertained, you can get it all from Roblox.■

ROBLOX

314

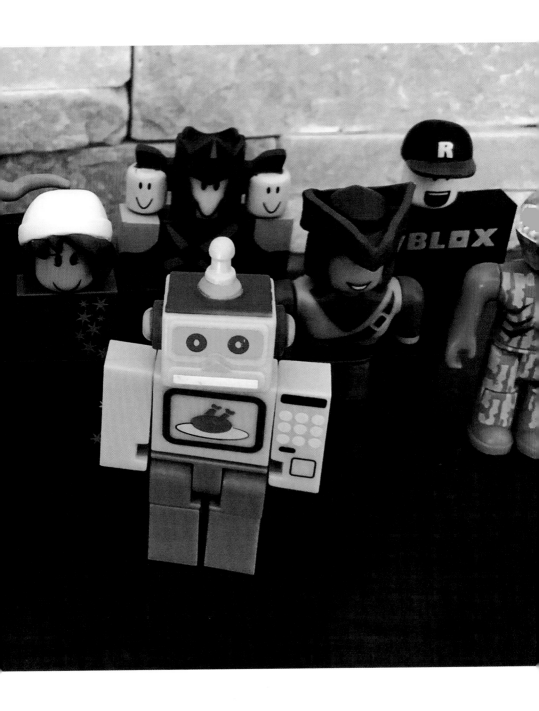

Top Roblox Players

You want to know which Roblox players are at the top and the most famous in the game?

You want to know where they go and what they do while they are there, too, don't you?

It's tough catching these top players in-game, and even more difficult getting in the same game worlds as them. You never quite know where they are if you are not a friend with them on the game. If you are lucky though, you might come across one of these elite players randomly and get a chance to go against them or play on the same team as them.

The coolest part about this is that many of these players also have YouTube channels, so if you can find them then you have a chance of being shown in their videos.

Isn't that pretty awesome?
We thought it was!

If you're ready to learn more about the most popular players in the game and where to find them then follow us!

We put together our list of leading Roblox players according to their total page view count. These are the elite Roblox players, and chances are good you've heard of at least a few of these top players before. They're some of the most entertaining players, have the biggest group of followers and some of the most sought-after players in Roblox too!

Take a look through our list and see what games each of these elite players frequents the most.

Alexnewtron – MeepCity

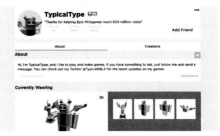

TypicalType – Epic Minigames

Nikillis – Murder Mystery 2

Cindering – ROBLOX High School

Callmehbob – Royale High

Vurse – Speed Run 4

Stickmasterluke – Natural Disaster Survival

Prisman – Assassin

DemSkittlesDoee – Robloxian Life

Onett – Bee Swarm Simulator

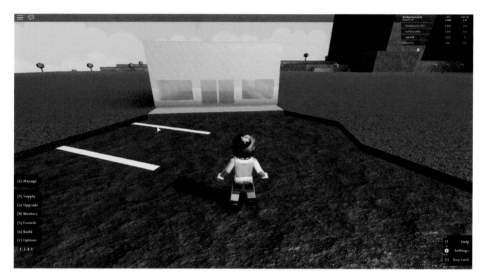

Use this list as the most likely place these Roblox players will be. Of course, they play on other game worlds as well. If you really want to follow and get a chance to play with these gamers, send out a friend request and see what they say!

There are also many YouTube players that play the game just to show off their Roblox moves. If you are looking for these types of players, then you have come to the right place because we've assembled a list of the top Roblox YouTubers available today. With our list you can go online and see their different channels for yourself. Take a look and see why they're the top YouTubers in the Roblox community!

YouTubers That Play Roblox

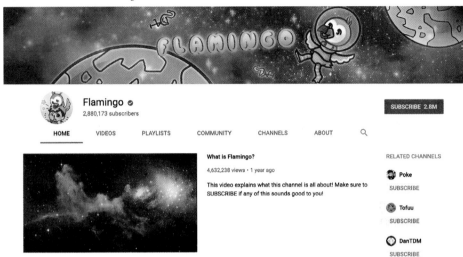

Flamingo — This is a fun, kid-oriented channel that welcomes one and all to come in and have a great time. You can watch them do unboxing of some pretty awesome toys but playing Roblox and making creative movies using their favorite Roblox game worlds is what they like to do most.

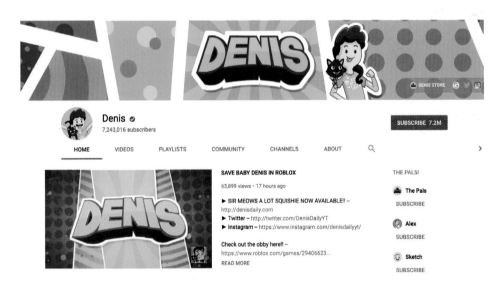

Denis — All of the games that Denis plays are kid friendly, which makes him an ideal choice to go with if you are worried about not being able to watch it because of your parents. No worries! You probably already know about this awesome Roblox player and have probably already seen him play!

Screenshots: Roblox® ™ & © 2019 Roblox Corporation

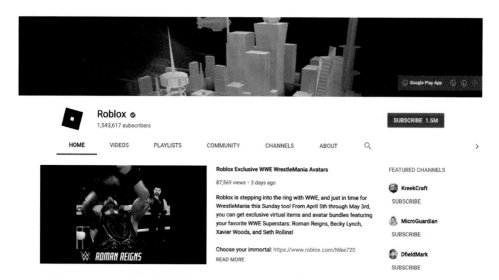

ROBLOX! — Of course, they'd be on this list because you want to make sure that you can watch the developers in action when they have their avatars running around the worlds and popping into each of the games that players make! Pretty awesome if you run into one of them!

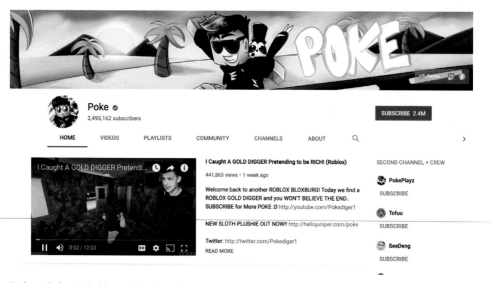

Poke — Poke is a kid himself, so he is definitely going to be creating some awesome content for the rest of us to watch. I haven't been able to see him around the game much but if you do see him, make sure to say hey! You also should check out his channel to find some of the awesome builds he's made and games he's played.

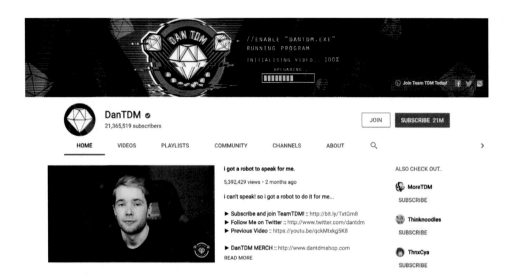

DanTDM — He is well known throughout many gaming platforms and probably one of the best YouTubers to watch for quality Roblox content. When you want to see Roblox in action, he is one of the ones to watch! Dan has a pretty big following base and he does do other things, but he is still known to stop in on Roblox from time to time.

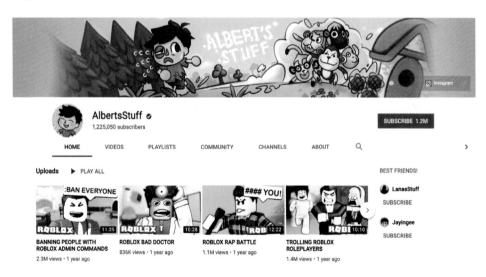

AlbertsStuff — He is pretty weird, but he has a lot of friends and he makes some of the best videos. If you are looking for a good laugh and something entertaining to watch on YouTube, then he is going to be the one to check out. You can either visit him on YT or you can check out some of the links he has put up on Roblox. He has a community that you can be a part of when you find him on the game.

ROBLOX

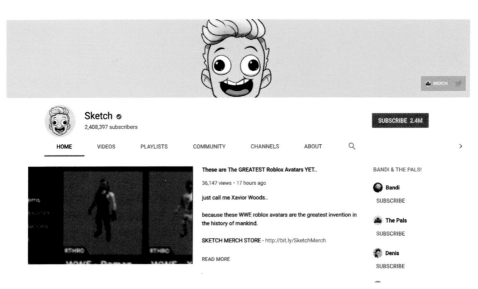

Sketch — They make some of the coolest things on their YouTube channel. They love the Roblox car games, so watch for these popular YouTubers in leading driving games. Not only that, but they have a pretty good way to make their avatars look their best. Colorful and fun, this is a great player to watch.

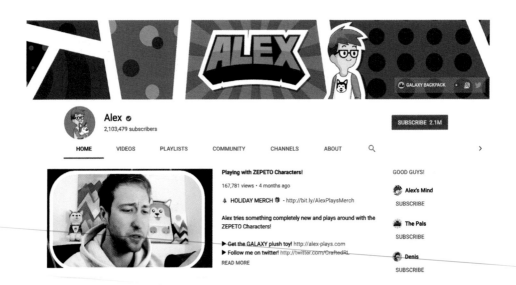

Alex — One of Alex's coolest features of his channel is that he makes a lot of Roblox music videos for you to check out. His videos are creative, entertaining and give you a new way to enjoy the Roblox universe when you're bored. He does play the game too, and you can sometimes catch him recording videos while playing, but the music vids he puts up are the best.

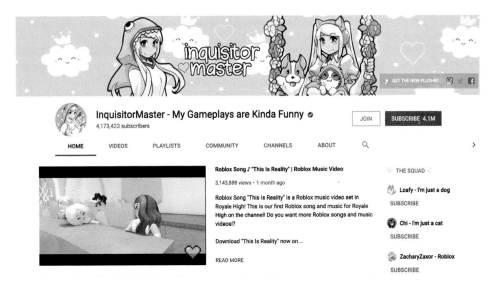

Inquisitormaster — She is known for her pretty videos that put you in the decision-making box of what she should wear, or what dance she should go to, or even what date she should go with. This is one of the girls that really likes storytelling and having her followers help her every step of the way. She loves playing dress up and fantasy games on Roblox, so you might be able to find her there!

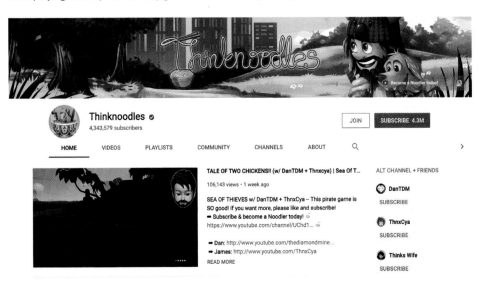

Thinknoodles — Everyone likes a little food and fun and when you are watching Thinknoodles, you can get a giant dose of both. Enjoy all that comes from the excitement that this YouTuber brings. While he does play a lot of other games online, you can catch him playing (and cooking) on Roblox from time to time. Check out some of his videos to see where he visits most often.

ROBLOX

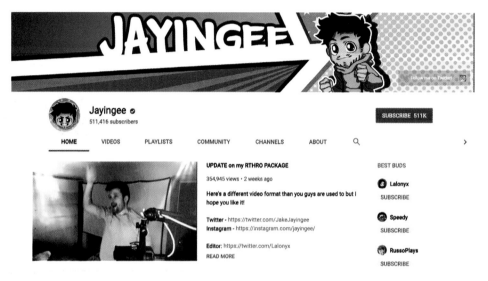

Jayingee — He is a player of Roblox that loves to show off and have a good time. He has released some cool world creations of his own but prefers to play in the other player's games. He cuts out parts from other videos and then puts them together to create funny clips that are worth watching. Just look at his YouTube intro video for an idea.

 PrestonMobile
1,461,169 subscribers

SUBSCRIBE 1.4

HOME VIDEOS PLAYLISTS COMMUNITY CHANNELS ABOUT

I CHEATED! BOY vs GIRL ROBLOX HOLE IN THE WALL CHALL...

2,058,816 views · 3 months ago

I CHEATED! BOY vs GIRL ROBLOX HOLE IN THE WALL
CHALLENGE! with PrestonRoblox
SUBSCRIBE for more videos! https://bit.ly/2znnKsV

FRIENDS
Brianna - http://bit.ly/Sub2Brianna

READ MORE

✓ MORE CHANNELS!

Preston
SUBSCRIBE

TBNRFrags
SUBSCRIBE

PrestonPlayz
SUBSCRIBE

PrestonMobile — He doesn't just play on Roblox, you can catch him playing some of the other games out there like Minecraft and Fortnite. You might be able to catch him in any of those games, as well! He is a leader in the Roblox industry when it comes to showcasing some of the best Roblox moments and worlds to test out.

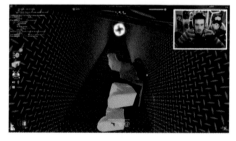

Watching leading Roblox YouTubers is a fun and exciting way to enjoy Roblox and the creative energy it has to offer. If you have the pleasure of finding one of these leading creators in one of the games, then it might be time to say hello and you could even get featured in one of their videos if you're lucky enough! Though it's tough to say exactly when these elite players will be on, or what they'll be doing on Roblox, using our guide above can help you find some of them.

If you are thinking about having fun in Roblox, you can also consider recording your game time and putting it up. Everyone likes to watch you go into different games and check out the different things. Let everyone else see how you have fun with Roblox!

Of course, you don't have to. Creating videos is just one way players enjoy the game. You can definitely have fun on Roblox regardless of whether or not you are a YouTuber or a top player within the game.

Roblox is designed to offer fun for all, whether you're a builder, a video creator or a player testing out all the different games released by everyone else. Roblox is a game that welcomes everyone, and it's a blast no matter what you do with your time in the different worlds.

Are you ready to see all that is waiting for you inside Roblox?

Want to know if you can become one of the most visited characters in the game?

There is only way to make sure that this is something that happens!

You have to keep playing to see where it brings you! The more you play, the more you will be noticed in the game and the more fun you are going to have!

RainbowsYT

Fun

GOLD3NGLARE

ROBLOX

Roblox Toy Line

Roblox isn't just a video game any longer, it's also a line of toys for you to play with in real life. That means that serious Roblox fans can pick up additional toys to collect and to enjoy every day. If you want Roblox toys of your own you can enjoy everything from small characters to plushes, blind bags and codes that you get in a box.

Take a look through the many different options out there for you to bring home. You might find somethings you didn't know they had, some things you already have or learn something new about this awesome toy line!

Roblox toys are widely available and it's likely they're available at different stores near you! Online shopping is another option you can use to obtain Roblox toys easily and is the only option if you want some of the older toys not available for sale any longer.

How do you keep track of all these toys that are coming and going from the shelves and into your room?

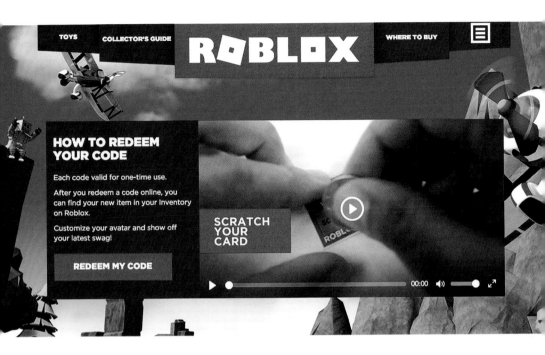

COLLECTOR'S GUIDE

If you're someone that enjoys being able to collect everything that is out there, then you want to make sure that you're choosing the right toys for the collection.

Roblox has a Collector's Guide that you can grab right off their website.

This Collector's Guide allows you to collect all of the toys and check them off as you get them. This is something that can provide the player with a way to collect them all and make sure that they get the best products and really keep the collecting going.

They might add more as they update the list with time, but this is something that you would have to check back later on.

WHAT TOYS ARE AVAILABLE?

If you want to know the selection of toys that you can choose from, then you are in luck! We built a list of the many different options available, so you can look down and see every type of toy available currently.

The Tool Box

This awesome tool box has the space needed to keep the toys that you are playing with in the right places. Never have to worry about not knowing where to put your guys. Specially made with spaces just for them, it is the perfect size!

Playsets

There are whole playsets that you can choose and use when it comes to putting down some cash on toys that you can have fun with. They come with the characters, the accessories, props and the entire setting that you need to enjoy playing. Some of the options that come with these sets include Fashion Famous, Zombie Attack and Operation TNT.

Mix and Match with These Sets!

When you want a set that comes with some of the coolest items and characters, then these are what you would get. You can take their parts off and move them between the characters in the pack or even mix and match with the other packs. Some of the options are: Robot Riot, Punk Rockers, Days of Knights and Superstars.

Vehicles

These vehicles have just what you need to re-create those cool scenes that you probably play in many of the games. You can find that they also come with a character that can go in the vehicle of choice. With everything from a shark and duck floaty to an army Jeep or Sheriffs car, you're sure to have a good time.

Assortment Sets

With six different characters, the fun is never going to end. You can find yourself having a great time while you mix and match with these guys. The sets come with a different guy that goes along with the main theme. Some of the themes you can choose from include: Citizens of Roblox, Masters of Roblox and Champions of Roblox.

There are also assortment sets that come with four figures instead of six. You can choose either one. Each provides the characters and their accessories that come with them depending on the theme of the set. Neverland Lagoon is a popular 4 set.

Core Figures

These are just figures that you can purchase on their own. If you want to grab a character without the extra playset, but that comes with a code and an accessory, then these little guys are the ones you would get.

Some of the core figures that are being offered include:

- Circuit Breaker
- Captain Rampage
- Bride
- Flame Guard General
- Frost Empress
- Headless Horseman
- Hunted Vampire
- Hang Glider
- MeepCity Fisherman
- Mr. Bling Bling
- Pixel Artist
- The Golden Bloxy Award
- Shark Bite Surfer

Keep in mind that this is not all of them. There are many different characters that go along with the core figures you can grab. You can get them right in the blind bags that are handed out, or you can go with a box or even just purchase them in their own box.

ROBLOX

Game Packs

There are also whole game packs that you can grab depending on what it is that you're looking to use them for. They come with the character, as well as the accessories for the specific scene that they are a part of. Some of the game packs you can find include Mad Studio, Innovation Labs, Roblox High School, Chicken Simulator, Mount of the Gods, Fantastic Frontier, Where's the Baby, Work at a Pizza Place, and Top Roblox Runway Model.

Mystery Figures

There are the blind boxes or bags that were mentioned before with the single figures. These are the figures that you can get but they come in series. The series will depend on what is currently being offered at the store that you go to. The characters that you are able to get will depend on the series that you have.

The box comes with one character, one accessory, one virtual item code and one checklist for the blind box series that you can collect.

PRODUCT FEATURES OF THE TOYS

When you purchase the toys, you can benefit from what that have to offer because almost every toy you get has these features, which brings even more fun and games with them when you make a purchase.

Removable Parts

The parts on the toys are removable. You can pop them on and off and mix and match the pieces and parts. If you want a princess that has a robot leg and an armored arm, you're able to get just that from her look and feel. This is something that is pretty awesome when it comes to adding to your collection but being able to mix and match the parts to create your own unique character, kind of like how you can do with your avatar online.

The possibilities are endless when it comes to what you can and cannot put together!

They Come with Codes

There is a code with every single toy that you purchase. This code provides you with a way to cash in on some pretty cool swag. You are able to jump online to your Roblox account and then enter the code on your account.

ROBLOX

You just follow the link on the paper with the code to redeem, type in the code that you have, and your character will be able to use the items that you got with the toys that they were given. It is easy, and it is a great way to grab some new items for your avatar without having to purchase Robux in order to do so. Every character comes with something different, so you have to collect them all in order to cash out with them!

QUICK INSTRUCTIONS FOR REDEEMING YOUR CODES

> Scratch the covering over the code off gently

> Log into your Roblox account before you redeem the code

> Go to the Redemption Page for the Toy Codes on the website

> Type in your code that is provided to you on the paper exactly as you see it

> Your item is then added to your personal inventory

Accessories are a Must!

When you want to keep the action going, even with your toys, they all come with accessories that can be added to the little people that hold them. When you mix and match their body parts, you can also mix and match their accessories.

Each one comes with something different and depending on which wave of toys you get, something new is always coming out with different characters.

Use the collector's checklist to make sure that you are collecting all of the necessary characters and getting all of their awesome items along with them! This helps everyone stay on track and purchase the right toys and accessories! Plus, you can take advantage of some of the coolest online gear from the codes they provide!

Some of the places you can go to buy these and other great Roblox toys include:

- Target
- eBay
- Amazon
- GameStop
- Ace Hardware Stores
- Bi Mart
- Best Buy
- Claire's
- Calendar Holdings
- CVS
- FYE
- Hot Topic
- Journey's Kids
- Hobbytown
- Kmart
- Mills Fleet Farm
- Learning Express
- Sears
- Walgreens
- Wegmans
- Walmart
- True Value Stores
- Value Drug

Keep in mind that these places are all located in the United States. For those that want to purchase them outside of the country, you'd have to find out where they are being sold where you are from.

ROBLOX

SOME OF THE COOLEST TOYS TO COLLECT

You can use our cool checklist to check off those toys that you already have off this list, but remember, there are always new toys and models coming out, so it is important that you update your list whenever you can and try to collect them all!

Item to Collect	Check Here
ROBLOX TOOL BOX	
MIX & MATCH SETS	
DAYS OF KNIGHTS	
DISCO MADNESS	
FASHION ICONS	
PUNK ROCKERS	
ROBOT RIOT	
STYLZ SALON & SPA	
SUPERSTARS	
PLAYSETS	
FASHION FAMOUS	
HEROES OF ROBLOXIA	
OPERATION TNT	
ZOMBIE ATTACK	

Item to Collect	Check Here
VEHICLES	
APOCOLYPSE RISING 4X4	
JAILBREAK: SWAT UNIT	
NEIGHBORHOOD OF ROBLOXIA: PATROL CAR	
SHARKBITE: DUCK BOAT	
THE ABOMINATOR	
4-PACK ASSORTMENTS	
NEVERLAND LAGOON	
6-PACK ASSORTMENTS	
CHAMPIONS OF ROBLOX	
CITIZENS OF ROBLOX	
LEGENDS OF ROBLOX	
MASTER OF ROBLOX	

Item to Collect	Check Here	Item to Collect	Check Here
CORE FIGURES		HUNTED VAMPIRE	
ARMS DEALER		LORD UMBERHALLOW	
BANDIT		MAD GAMES: ADAM	
PARKOUR RUNNER		MATT DUSEK	
CAPTAIN RAMPAGE		MEEPCITY FISHERMAN	
BRIDE		MR. BLING BLING	
CAR CRUSHER		NEVERLAND LAGOON: CROWN COLLECTOR	
CIRCUIT BREAKER			
CREZAK: THE LEGEND		NINJA ASSASSIN: YIN CLAN MASTER	
EMERALD DRAGON MASTER			
DESIGN IT: TEIYIA		NINJA ASSASSIN: YANG CLAN MASTER	
FALLEN ARTEMIS			
CROC		PHANTOM FORCES: GHOST	
FLAME GUARD GENERAL		QUEEN OF THE TREE LANDS	
FROST GUARD GENERAL		PIXEL ARTIST	
FROST EMPRESS		ROBLOX HIGH SCHOOL: SPRING BREAK	
GHOST FORCES: PHANTOM			
HEADLESS HORSEMAN		ROBLOX SKATING RINK	
HANG GLIDER		ROYALE HIGH SCHOOL: ENCHANTRESS	
THE WHISPERING DREAD			
LA HOVERBOARDER		SKYBOUND ADMIRAL	
		SHARKBITE SURFER	

ROBLOX

Item to Collect	Check Here	Item to Collect	Check Here
THE CLOUDS: FLYER		ROBLOX HIGH SCHOOL	
THE GOLDEN BLOXY AWARD		SORO'S FINE ITALIAN DINING	
VORLIAS		TOP ROBLOX RUNWAY MODEL	
WILD STARR		WHERE'S THE BABY!	
GAME PACKS		SWORDBURST ONLINE	
CLUB BOATES		THE PLAZA: JET SKIERS	
CHICKEN SIMULATOR		WORK AT A PIZZA PLACE	
FANTASTIC FRONTIER		**MYSTERY FIGURES**	
INNOVATION LABS		SERIES 1	
GAME DEV LIFE		SERIES 2	
MAD STUDIO		SERIES 3	
PRISON LIFE		SERIES 4	
MOUNT OF THE GODS		SERIES 5	

If you're serious about collecting all the toys, you can go down this list and see which of these characters you need!

You will also want to consider keeping the checklist that you get for the blind boxes. You can check off every single character that you get from the series. Collect them all today and show them off!

Everyone wants to show off their awesome characters and now that you have a checklist, you can be sure that you are able to do just that!

Awesome Events Near You!

There are also many awesome events that come and go from the stores near you. You can check the website where you can redeem the codes and find out if they are going to be at one of the stores near you!

This is a great way to get more from Roblox because they sometimes offer some of the best extras and hand out fun games, crafts and items for players, just like you, to use!

If you're looking for a cool new collectible to add to your home and you're a fan of Roblox, there is a bunch of Roblox swag to collect and it will look great in your room! Build up your collection, play with your toys, mix and match your characters and enjoy all the Roblox themed goodness.

Not only do you get awesome toys to play with, but the code gives you a bit extra to use while you're on your Roblox account and you get to collect something that is completely awesome.

Roblox has so many toys out there for you to make use of. Make sure to keep the fun going when it comes to collecting them all for yourself! Look at all that they have for you to make use of today!

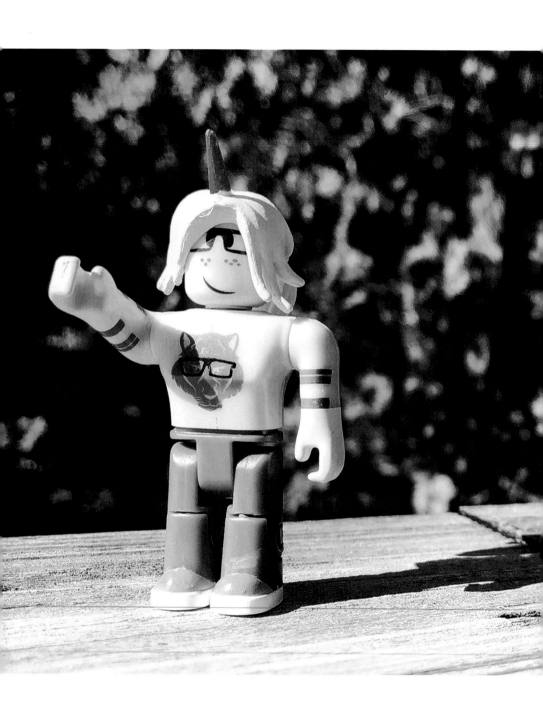

Conclusion

Roblox is one of the most exciting, fascinating and open games out there.

You can find yourself creating worlds of your own to share with the others at one point, and trying out games that make you want to play for hours on end at another. You even open up new social interactions and create opportunities for meeting new friends and taking vacations away from the home you live in through a virtual world.

However, the best part of Roblox is the fact that you can be your own creator. You can create and enjoy being able to offer something that is made by you, and that's just as awesome as you are.

Of course, if you are not someone that is into creating, then you are more than welcome to go into the game and check out what others have made and just have fun with it. No one is making you take part in any area of Roblox you aren't excited about. That's what's great, you're free to do what you like in this online experience.

When it comes to playing the game, it should always be your goal to enjoy your time with the game and to just enjoy the experience.

Are you ready to play?

What if you want to be the one that is making the creative game?

You can absolutely do that if it's something you're interested in! There really are no limitations to what you can and cannot do when you are a part of the Roblox community of players and developers.

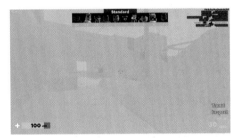

Now that you have an idea of what you can expect inside the Roblox game and what comes with it, as well as what is new with it, it's time to start exploring it for yourself. Roblox is definitely a game you're going to want to spend some time playing around with. That's because it's a unique experience, and a game everyone should try even if they decide not to stick with it.

Roblox is a fun-filled game that provides everyone with the fun that they want and the excitement that they deserve at the same time. With a way to customize your character, many different types of games to visit, a way to create your own game or world and even a way to make some actual cash, Roblox is a game that's worth spending some time on.

We've offered so many different things to you, including tips, tricks, tutorials, some fun trivia, cool avatars and so much more in this guide. Now it's up to you to make sure you're taking advantage of all those resources, and most importantly experiencing Roblox for the entertaining game that it is.

Hopefully, you now understand more about what it means to make the most of the Roblox world. Top creators get to feel like celebrities and to showcase their talent in a big way, and who knows, that could be you.

When you are looking at the many ways you can build on your own game, we have shown you some tips and tricks for really making that game you build stand out more than the others. You want to be the best, don't you?

Just think outside the box to create something unique and exciting that others will respond to. What is something that no one else has ever done before? What is something that appeals to you and your friends?

You can create a group and get everyone together to have a great time playing and creating a game if you don't want to be the creator of the game entirely. The Creators of Roblox believe that making new worlds and creating in general should be fun to do. So, if building with all of your friends on your next creation is what you're interested in, the creators of Roblox want to make that happen for you.

Read through our section about creating a game of your own, and our tips to help you make a game that actually sells as well. Roblox games are an excellent opportunity to earn real world money if you create something people truly love. There's a whole world out there, start creating and putting your creations out to everyone around you so that you can show off all that you can do.

By taking some time to expand on what is out there and offer something completely unique and your own, the creators are hoping to give something different back to the community of players. That's one of the reasons that Roblox is so successful. The company relies on its players to supply new and exciting content, which has resulted in some very impressive creations over the years.

Screenshots: Roblox® ™ & © 2019 Roblox Corporation

ROBLOX

We have had a great time being able to show you some of the most awesome things that make Roblox special to us and millions of others. We took the time to assemble all this information, to help you have as much fun with Roblox as we have over the years. We made this book with the idea that our readers would spread this information with others as well. Share with your friends, share with your neighbors and keep the book handy. You never know when you might need some of these tips again.

Everyone that has ever tried Roblox knows how much fun it can be and how much fun you can have whether you are creating a new world or if you are creating something unique to you and your friends just for fun, or if you just want to bounce around from game to game. The choice is yours. That is one of the best things about this game.

Not only that, but it is FREE to play, which is different from the many other games out there.

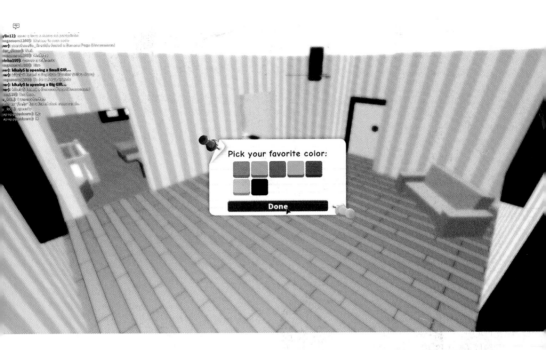

You don't need money or Robux in order to play. You just need some time, the ability to have fun, an idea of what types of games you like to play and some creativity to design and build new worlds that players will want to come and enjoy.

What are you waiting for?

We welcome you to spend some time on this game and even try to become one of the top creators out there. You want to have a great time while playing and through the use of the fun and games that this game has, so get on and create. Roblox won't stand in your way, and it's one of the few online creative engines that lets you design anything you like without stepping on your creativity.

Robloxians United! Roblox is waiting for all of your creative minds to come together to create thrilling new experiences for everyone. This online world is made by the players for the players, and it really shows. Get started with the

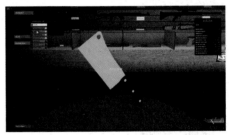

game today, and experience everything that it has to offer. You won't be sorry that you did. Roblox was made for players like you!